Something in the Blood

# Something in the Blood

## The Underground World of Today's Vampires

**JEFF GUINN**

**with Andy Grieser**

THE SUMMIT PUBLISHING GROUP

THE SUMMIT PUBLISHING GROUP

One Arlington Centre, 1112 East Copeland Road, Fifth Floor
Arlington, Texas 76011

Printed in the United States of America.

00  99  98  97  96    010    5  4  3  2  1

**Library of Congress Cataloging-in-Publication Data**


Guinn, Jeff.
    Something in the blood : the underground world of today's vampires
/ By Jeff Guinn with Andy Grieser.
        p.  cm.
    ISBN 1-56530-209-5  (cloth)
        1. Vampires in literature.  2. Vampires.  I. Grieser, Andy.  II. Title
PN56.V3G85  1996
809'.93375—dc20                                        96-10104
                                                        CIP

*Cover design by David Sims*
*Book design by John Baird*

This book is dedicated to Jane Holt.

It's also dedicated to Andy,
because it's his first.

# Contents

*Who among you understands it?*
*Bloody mouths and bloody hands are all you know.*
*But soon you'll know the vampire . . .*

"VAMPIRE"
MICHAEL SMITH
FLYING FISH CD FF70404

# Preface

You were right. There were times when you were younger that a movie or book about vampires scared you. Those nights, you cowered under your blankets, feeling certain a vampire was skulking outside your window, or at least was nearby. Your mother always said you were being silly, that there were no such things as real vampires.

She was wrong. We've spent months traveling the country, meeting real vampires. You're about to meet them, too. As you do, at various times you'll probably feel excited, shocked, thrilled, repelled, and, if you buy too much into the vampires of movies and modern best-selling novels, maybe you'll even be a little disappointed in some of them.

Not too disappointed, though. True, none of the vampires who walk this earth like the rest of us can transform themselves into bats. They aren't afraid of garlic or driven away by crucifixes. They certainly aren't turned into dust by direct exposure to sunlight. Living, breathing vampires don't have to mug victims in back alleys, either. They usually don't have trouble finding "donors," the vampire term for people willing to let someone else drink their blood. And forget entirely the myth of vampires getting blood through any other violent means. That's made-up stuff from books and movies.

But there are some real vampires who do sleep in coffins, some who hate the sunlight, some who think they'll live forever, and others who believe they've gained superhuman powers. We met a few vampires who drink blood every week, others who do their blood-drinking once a month, still others who have no set schedule of blood-drinking at all. There are even vampires who disdain blood-drinking, preferring to drain "lifeforce" or "energy" from unsuspecting victims.

The truth is that there's no single cookie-cutter type of vampire any more than there's just one generic category of American, or Christian, or Republican. To get the most out of this book, purge all the vampire stereotypes from your mind. Open up to hearing from men and women who truly believe they have the right to take someone else's blood or lifeforce to enhance their own. They're all different ages, from all different backgrounds, and each pursues his or her vampire existence in a unique way. How unique? Prepare yourself. No matter how normal they may appear in everyday situations—and some *do* appear to be so very, very normal—nobody becomes a practicing vampire without taking long, frequent walks on the stranger side of life.

Again, focus on this simple, staggering fact: Vampires do exist. They're as real as you are, and some of them may not be too far away as you read this. After considerable investigation, we found them all around the country, from a dingy Seattle apartment to a snazzy Orlando suburb and many other unexpected places in between. Most were young, a few were older. Gender made no difference—both males and females find themselves involved in what many vampires call, in sort of verbal shorthand, The Life.

If you're easily frightened, don't read on, because afterward you will be like we are. Now, in grocery stores or at baseball games, amid the car-pool moms at elementary schools and the downtown workers hurrying home before nightfall, anywhere people congregate, we can't help wondering: Which ones are vampires?

And know this: Everything you'll read here is true. We have each interview on tape, and the photographs were provided by the vampires themselves. In only a few instances, noted in the afterword, we've changed names at the vampires' requests to conceal their everyday identities, or else left out some details to protect the vampires' families or loved ones. As you'll see, all the vampires were extraordinarily open about how they became what they are. Often, they were eager to dispel myths. They *want* you to understand what they do and why they do it. We've tried not to add too many of our own opinions about each of them, though you'll certainly form yours. These interviews, as presented in *Something in the Blood*, come directly from the vampires to you.

How many real vampires are out there? Nobody's sure, though on the pages that follow you'll meet some industrious followers of The Life who are constantly doing surveys to try to find out. Of one thing be certain: We could have met and talked to hundreds if we had wanted to. The vampires in this book were selected as a good cross section of the broad vampire spectrum.

They include one or two who consider themselves vampires even though they don't drink blood, some who follow The Life because of vampire sex, and others who think sex has nothing at all to do with being a vampire. Several don't even like the term "vampire." One prefers "dark angel" and another, "blood-drinker." The first interview is with a young woman who tried The Life, then decided she didn't believe in it after all.

Chapters where we introduce you to these real vampires alternate with informational chapters. To understand who you are reading about, it's important to learn how the whole vampire legend has evolved over the centuries, and why it continues to fascinate so many people in so many places.

Let's begin. If you're reading this at night, go lock the doors and turn on all the lights. Later, as you try to fall asleep, remember your mother telling you there aren't any real vampires.

Sorry, Mom. There are.

Jeff Guinn with Andy Grieser
Fort Worth, Texas
June 1996

*"I've avoided actual blood-drinking, because I think that would bring me too close. To do what I do, I need to keep my objectivity."*

MARTIN RICCARDO

# Prologue

The vampire underground is tightly knit. Members thousands of miles apart who have never met in person may have written each other letters, read about each other in publications, or talked on the phone. For example, almost everyone we interviewed knew about Martin Riccardo and his Vampires Studies organization in Chicago. Blood-drinkers and vampire fans alike hailed him as one of the nation's foremost authorities on vampirism. We were skeptical until we met him.

Over the years, Riccardo's modest home in a Chicago suburb has become a gathering place for visitors who either practice The Life themselves or else are just fascinated by it. He gets far more mail than he can answer from people who want him to put them in touch with vampires. A professional hypnotist by trade, Riccardo, a stocky man in his middle forties, became interested in vampirism as a college student when a visiting lecturer, Leonard Wolf, discussed his book, *A Dream of Dracula*.

By 1977, Riccardo was giving lectures on the history of vampirism. He began publishing *The Journal of Vampirism*, which brought him to the attention of the very individuals he was lecturing and writing about. Riccardo has since written several books, done years of tough, objective research, and soon will publish his latest book, *Liquid Dreams of Vampires*, which explores the subconscious power of the vampire image. He has even hosted a series of vampire conventions in Chicago.

Though he deserves his own full chapter, our lengthy interviews with Riccardo will be represented by his comments in several other chapters, including those on the vampire marketplace, vampire sexuality, and the vampire in modern society. As a source of accurate information, his credentials are impeccable.

While we will provide addresses of several individuals in *Something in the Blood*, Riccardo's won't be among them. Because of the volume of mail he already receives, he asked that we not print his address. But we suspect that if you try to contact him in care of Christine Darque, or Vlad the rock and roller, or Michelle and David Belanger of Shadowfox Publications, they'll probably pass your letters along to Riccardo if they think what you've written is sufficiently interesting.

Riccardo, who says he has never tried blood-drinking himself, hopes to eventually persuade the public that 99 percent of all vampires or blood-drinkers aren't evil or even dangerous.

"If you see a vampire person of any kind on the street, you might be apprehensive about going up to them because they're dressed in black, they sometimes have strange makeup, sometimes body-piercing, sometimes fangs," Riccardo said. "Yes, they can be a little intimidating. But many have come to my home, spent time with my wife and me, and the people we've gotten to know are very nice people, friendly, easy to get along with, just like any normal human being."

Riccardo helped us get in touch with several of the vampires we interviewed. A few written about extensively in this book only agreed to cooperate because of his support for the project. We're grateful for his help. And now that Riccardo has been introduced, he would insist, properly, that it's time to let you get on with reading about vampires.

Martin Riccaudo and Wife

*"I don't know, it was just a feeling. . .I'm a vampire, and that's all there is to it. If people are going to suck off me, then I'm going to turn it around and do it to them."*

LIRIEL MCMAHON

# 1
## *Liriel*

L iriel McMahon certainly didn't look like a vampire, or at least what most people would imagine a vampire might look like. At twenty-four, she seemed almost waiflike, a tiny young woman with pale skin, close-cropped, curly red hair, normal teeth—no long, sharp fangs!—and a slender body swathed in a baggy black tunic and long black skirt. Only a black leather, metal-studded motorcycle jacket and heavy, steel-tipped brogans lent the slightest hint of menace to her appearance. Entering a fancy downtown Seattle restaurant, in fact, Liriel looked more like a street kid about to panhandle diners than what she really was—the founder/director/one-woman staff of Seattle's Vampirism Research Institute, and someone who had recently abandoned The Life after a long experiment with vampirism herself.

"I wear the jacket to keep people away," Liriel explained as she sat down, her voice soft enough to require careful listening. "I don't have a car, so I ride the bus every day. At night, some of the other people who ride the bus scare me. I try to wear tough-looking clothes so they'll leave me alone."

During the days when she made a regular weekly ritual of blood-drinking, Liriel probably could have frightened off the toughest street thugs by identifying herself as a vampire. She had, she soon admitted, tried The Life in self-defense as much as anything else. And even though she no longer drinks blood or believes there are immortal vampires with superpowers, Liriel still keeps up her extensive research, hoping to discover why so many people are attracted to vampirism.

"Among the people I've written to who thought they were vampires, I've found a lot of them felt abandoned as children, or their parents left them alone to do their own thing, or they just felt unloved," Liriel said. "A few even described suffering child abuse. Rarely was there a case where people said, 'Yeah, my family relations were great, we all get along.'"

With the benefit of hindsight, Liriel thinks her own eight-year flirtation with vampirism fits that pattern.

"In all these surveys, I was learning about other people, but I was also learning about myself," she agreed. "I know now what happened to me is pretty typical of what happens to a lot of people, and because of that I don't feel so alone anymore."

Liriel was born in Los Angeles. Her mother cared for convalescents. Her father worked in the theater as a set designer, dancer, and choreographer. Liriel's father named her after a character in a science fiction novel. Together with her parents and older sister, she soon moved to Sacramento, where she had miserable experiences in public schools.

"I was a loner kid, and I'd spend most of my time in our backyard," Liriel recalled. "I wasn't close to Laura, my sister. She was eight years older, an extrovert, very gregarious. Then my parents got divorced when I was twelve, and my father moved back down to L.A. I've kind of lost track of him. But before he left, he got me the first books I really loved, *The Chronicles of Narnia*. I must've read them about fifteen times each."

Liriel hated school: "There's all these kids, and they're testing you. They called me 'Medusa' because I had long, wild hair. What was I going to do? Was I going to ignore them, or call them a name back, or punch them out?"

Her mother's solution was to take Liriel out of school completely after the sixth grade. At home, the child lived in her own fantasy world, writing a five-hundred-page novel as her first postschool project. But it was a book other than her own, given to Liriel by a Sacramento girl who became her best friend, that turned Liriel into a budding vampire.

"I was riding my bicycle around the neighborhood one day, and Carmen was doing the same thing," Liriel remembered. "We were doing weird kind of approach-avoidance things, where we wouldn't talk to each other, but we'd stop for a while and stare. Finally she came over and said, 'What's your name?' And from then on we were just like bosom buddies. She liked horses, which was one of my favorite things at the time, and we began the vampire thing together."

Liriel was fifteen, already bored with a job at Taco Bell, when Carmen's family invited her to join them for dinner at a pizza parlor. Carmen brought two books along with her, and loaned Liriel one. It was Anne Rice's *Interview With the Vampire*, which had originally been published in 1976.

"I finished it the next day," Liriel said. "It was fascinating. The character of Lestat just jumped out at me. I went right to a used bookstore and looked for other vampire books. I got Bram Stoker's *Dracula*. That was the second one I read, and then a whole bunch of not-so-good ones. After I read them, though, vampirism became an obsession. My mother said if I was so interested, I ought to watch some movies on the subject, so we started getting all these cassettes. Well, obviously I'd fallen through the cracks of the social system, if you will, and I had started educating myself on things that I wanted to learn. It took a while. I read *Interview With the Vampire* in '87, and it wasn't until '91 that I was undergoing this transition into being a vampire."

For a while, Liriel had other interests besides vampirism. She spent much of the next three years playing bass in a Sacramento garage band when she wasn't working at Taco Bell, and briefly found her first real boyfriend. That relationship, as well as her band, was broken up by a family move to Seattle.

"My sister had married, they'd had a kid, and the husband was in the Coast Guard and got stationed in Seattle," she said. "My mother thought we'd take advantage of the Coast Guard paying for a moving truck and be, like, 'Cool, we're going to Seattle, too.' I was able to transfer to another Taco Bell up there. And I was looking forward to finding a new band in Seattle."

What Liriel found instead was crushing isolation. She moved in with her sister, who fought constantly with her husband.

"I'm pretty sensitive to strong emotions," Liriel said. "When there's someone angry, I'm like, 'I've got to get out of here.' It was a two-story house, and one room was underground, and I'm living there. It had a concrete floor with linoleum over it and a little bed and a stereo with one speaker. Because of what was going on upstairs, I spent most of my time in that room with my little heater on, trying to stay warm."

Besides working at Taco Bell, Liriel didn't have anything to do or anywhere to go.

"I was underage and had no vehicle or license and was living in West Seattle, which is quite a ways from downtown where there are underage clubs," she explained. "I was stuck. I'd end up walking around my neighborhood at night, Friday nights, you know, when you should be out having fun."

Vampirism, or at least pretending to be a vampire, gave Liriel her only break from drab workdays and tense nights at home.

"Since 1990 I'd been putting out this little vampire fanzine called *VAMPS*," she said. "There's this sort of vampire underground. People have newsletters and things. Booklets would go through the mail or be handed around person-to-person. They're called 'Friendship Books,' telling about the interests of the person, and that's how I started meeting other people, secondhand, through the mail. I started collecting vampire art pieces they'd draw or stories they'd send, and I decided to put it together into a publication, *VAMPS*, and sell it to other people. It was a dollar, real small, like about sixteen folded sheets or pages."

*VAMPS* didn't make Liriel enough money to quit her job at Taco Bell, but it gave her the chance to develop a second identity as a vampire named Gabrielle Padova, or, alternately, Gabrielle de Lioncourt, a name she said she took from an Anne Rice vampire novel.

"I was writing to one person in Michigan, his name was Alan, and I made up this fictional story about myself just to make an interesting letter," Liriel said. "The story I told was, 'I am a blood-drinker,' and I told him stuff about how I was doing the things, though in real life I wasn't doing them yet. But I was thinking about it. The idea was forming in my head. I thought you'd find someone that you'd take blood from, a friend or something, you'd use this razor, that kind of thing. And then as I found myself writing the story, I was getting more and more involved with the idea of it. I was feeling like, 'God, life sucks right now.' And that's when the transformation happened, right there."

⁂

Liriel picked up the story of her "transformation" the next afternoon at her home in a North Seattle suburb. Her house was a tiny, white frame structure, stuck in the center of a lower-middle-class warren densely populated by students who attended a nearby junior college.

Liriel rented the house with the help of a roommate, an older woman she described as "sort of an artist." The roommate briefly appeared once or twice while we talked, moving quickly between the kitchen and her bedroom. Inside, the house was starkly decorated—a few plants, cheap bookshelves sagging with books, which were a mix of Anne Rice and other vampire-theme novels and computer texts. Liriel had left Taco Bell behind and now worked for King County as a sort of computer troubleshooter.

The distinguishing features in the combination living room/dining room where Liriel settled in to talk were a fish tank populated by three gargantuan goldfish; a computer, printer, and copying machine Liriel used to write and print her Vampirism Reseach Institute—VRI for short—newsletter; and, in one corner, what appeared to be a large dead tree branch decorated with tiny fake blackbirds. It was the only decoration that might have made anyone suspect this was a former vampire's home.

Liriel was again dressed all in black, perhaps in the same clothes she'd worn to the restaurant the night before. In the pale winter sunlight that filtered in through the kitchen windows, her skin seemed almost translucent. She wore minimal makeup and no jewelry besides a stainless-steel watch and an ankh suspended from her neck by a chain. While she talked, though, Liriel's face would frequently flush, and she used very expressive hand gestures while explaining her first attempt at blood-drinking.

"I was keeping this journal. I guess I pretty much always keep a journal," Liriel said. "I wrote down what I was thinking about, which at the time was mostly about vampires and being a vampire."

She went into her bedroom and came back with a thick notebook. Opening it, she showed us various entries. Some she had signed at the bottom, and a few times signed both as Liriel

McMahon and Gabrielle Padova. In those cases, the handwriting for each signature was notably different.

On one particular night, Liriel said she found herself pausing from writing in her journal.

"I guess I identified so much with the vampire thing, the blood, that I went in the bathroom and found a razor, a straight-edge or something," she recalled. "I went back downstairs to my little room and started carving on the table there, and after a while I finally took the razor and sliced my thumb. And then I sat there looking at the blood, and finally I started spattering it on my note-book. I still have it in my diary here—see? Then I started think-ing, what am I doing? I went and put a Band-Aid on the cut."

Liriel couldn't put the moment out of her mind, though she tried.

"A couple weeks later I ended up doing the same thing," she said. "This time I ended up tasting the blood. And from there on I started doing this thing regularly on Friday or Saturday. It was like a sort of solace, a communion, if you will. There was no plea-sure at all, because it hurt. Here I am, cutting myself."

But she didn't stop. As a next step, Liriel wanted to try drink-ing another person's blood, but she didn't have the nerve to ask.

"I was just too much of an introvert to try to find someone else and say, 'Can I have your blood?'" she confessed.

Still, Liriel had now decided she was a vampire. She was deter-mined to look the part.

"Prior to moving to Seattle, I was dressed in blue jeans and T-shirts, stuff like that," she said. "When this started happening, I started buying black clothes and dressing in whatever black rags I could drag up."

About the same time, Liriel finally had company in her little room underground. Brian, a guy who'd played drums in her old

Sacramento band, left home and came north to Seattle. He moved into Liriel's house—there was extra room because her brother-in-law had been transferred to Kodiak, Alaska, leaving his wife and baby behind.

"Brian was eighteen, a year younger, but he had a vehicle," Liriel said. "So we had a way to go to clubs. We ended up spending every Friday and Saturday night at this one club in downtown Seattle called the Okay Hotel. It's still around, and it's changed a lot, but then it was just very much the punk thing, part of the grunge scene and all that. We'd get there, and I would hang out in the corners, being the black-dressed person that I was, smoking a clove cigarette and being a real watcher. I was still in this isolated phase, and the thing about teenagers is, they don't really talk to you unless they know you, and if they don't know you, it's kind of like, why bother? Brian would go in and meet these girls, and sometimes he'd bring over somebody he just met, and I'd be pretty pleasant."

Often, Brian took another girl back home along with Liriel. She didn't mind because her relationship with him was strictly platonic. Still, it hurt being alone. She missed her former—and still only—boyfriend back in Sacramento. After a few months, Brian went home to California, but Liriel kept going to the downtown Seattle clubs, taking the bus most of the way and having her mother pick her up when she was ready to come home.

"I still considered myself a vampire at this time, most definitely so," she said. "I was still sorting that out, and then I met my second boyfriend."

Liriel's new love interest was twenty-seven, to her mind an older man she had to impress.

"He was a player. He had several women and maybe even guys he was going out with, I don't know," she told us, her voice breaking a little at the memory. "I introduced myself to him as Gabrielle, that fictional character I'd made up. Later, on a date, I took him out to a restaurant and told him the truth. He thought the vampire thing was kind of silly and said, 'Yeah, right, vampires. You're not the only one.' And that was true. That punk scene, well, everyone was strange." ·

Liriel hoped for love but got herpes. When she confronted the boyfriend, he informed her he didn't want to see her anymore.

"Wooh, boy! That really did another number on my head," she sighed as she relived the disaster. "I wouldn't say that I was suicidal, but I felt like, I don't know, it was just a feeling—I'm a vampire, and that's all there is to it. If people are gonna suck off me, I'm just gonna turn it around and do it to them."

But she didn't. Liriel couldn't find the nerve to ask other people to be her blood donors, and soon she couldn't even ask it of herself. She was still working at Taco Bell, and washing dishes there caused the cuts on her thumb to be infected. There were no more weekend nights spent drinking her own blood.

"At that point, I'd sunk to an all-time low," she concluded. "I realized suddenly, 'Hey, wait a minute, I'm heading toward self-destruction. Why am I doing this? A real vampire is, well, something else, something I'm not, really.' So that's also why I stopped cutting myself."

Within three months, things got better. Liriel left her job at Taco Bell for a better one, though on a temporary basis, at the United Way. And she read another book, *Vampires Among Us*, by Rosemary Guiley. Though Liriel felt the author took up too much space offering her own opinions about people who thought they were vampires, she also took comfort in the fact that there seemed to be quite a few other men and women who shared her fascination with and experiments in vampirism.

"So in September of 1991, I started the VRI," she said. "I got various addresses from other vampire journals and started contacting people. I wanted to know why they believed what they did, why they did what they did."

After a false start, the *VRI News* began going out on a reasonably regular basis to a few dozen subscribers who paid barely enough to cover printing and postage (as of 1996, the cost was six dollars for six issues). Liriel sold some ads to help defray expenses, and in print interspersed her own reviews of vampire-themed books and movies with essays and other contributions from subscribers.

Her real love, though, was surveys she conducted. Some of the questions were charmingly simple: "Do you think that a Lestat-type vampire exists?" (Thirty-one respondents, or 72 percent, did.) Mostly, the surveys indicated those considering themselves vampires or vampire fans were young—almost always less than thirty.

"Most of the people I surveyed ranged anywhere from fourteen to twenty-nine," Liriel told us. "The oldest was fifty-four, the next oldest is forty-four."

The underground network that exists for professed vampires and those who simply like the idea of vampirism is widespread. Liriel's VRI activities even became known overseas. When she took a trip to Europe in 1994, she was profiled in Amsterdam-based *International Vampire* magazine, called *InterVamp* by loyal readers. In the story, Liriel introduced her concept of the "pseudovampire," which she defined as "a mortal human with a deceptive resemblance to a true vampire. These are people who claim to be vampires or who can display the traits of one...blood-drinking or blood-fascination, living at night or in the dark, dressing as a vampire, draining others of emotions or energies...sleeping in coffins, and so on."

At that time, Liriel still believed in real vampires, telling *InterVamp* that "most simply, a true vampire has all the proper trappings to fulfill its role, i.e., real fangs, immortality, being formerly dead, immunity to disease, supernatural powers and strength, and that ever-pervasive, mysterious aura of being the unknown. Unfortunately, I have never had the opportunity to meet a real vampire...the VRI does not profess to know and is not in the arena to debate their existence. The VRI is about vampirism, not vampires."

Liriel expanded on her belief in real vampires in a 1994 interview with *Erebus Rising*, a British underground magazine devoted to vampirism.

Citing seven years of research, Liriel offered the opinion that the modern vampire "is an immortal vampire, akin...to Lestat of current literature, where for instance you see more of the human in them as opposed to the monster with manners. The modern vampire is allowed to look really good, wear colors other than black, to fit into a crowd, and to be more daring and outright about what they are, etc. Another development of the twentieth century vampire...is the ground gained by female vampires."

She continued, "A whole other dimension was added in the mid- to late '80s that made the vampire an entirely more emotional, thoughtful, and even philosophical creature. This was initiated by Anne Rice's popular *Vampire Chronicles* (series of books), *The Vampire Lestat* most of all."

Liriel explained to *Erebus Rising* that she considered all the self-proclaimed vampires she'd met so far to be pseudovampires.

"The meaning of 'pseudo-' I use here is not meant as 'fake' or 'false' vampire, but more as a deceptive resemblance to the vampire for the simple reason that they are not the immortal type of vampire...usually a pseudovampire is a fan who has taken things to another level."

And that, she told us wryly in our interview just two years later, pretty much described herself.

&

Between 1991 and 1995, Liriel devoted much of her time to the Vampirism Research Institute. Though the *VRI News* never had more than fifty subscribers at any given time—after a while she gave up any hope of making a profit and gladly settled, most months, for breaking even—Liriel was able to correspond regularly over the years with several dozen individuals who claimed they were vampires. While she found herself doubting them—"I know how you can pretend to be a vampire in a letter, because I did it myself!"— she also continued to believe in the existence of the real thing.

"I kept feeling like, well, it's just got to be," she said. "How else would you explain the myth? And what about Anne Rice? I was actually thinking that maybe she wasn't making it all up."

Liriel had practically memorized *Interview With the Vampire* and Rice's sequels to that novel. Most of Rice's subsequent vampire books featured the character of Lestat, who absolutely fascinated the girl from Seattle.

"Lestat was a vampire. He had these supernatural powers, but he was very much someone who made moral judgments," Liriel said. "He seemed to prove vampires could have some feelings for mortal humans, too."

Liriel's VRI activities eventually brought her into contact with self-proclaimed vampires whose real-life activities were rumored to be crueler than Lestat's fictional carryings-on.

"There was this guy with a strange name, Tristram he was calling himself, and some of the VRI people started complaining he was writing them disturbing letters or something," she said. "So I wrote him and said, 'You better knock it off, people aren't digging it.' He wrote back that it was none of my business. I tried to cool him off by saying, 'Hey, I realize this is a game and you're playing out this part, but I think it's time to drop the act.' He said it wasn't an act."

Eventually, vampire underground scuttlebutt had Tristram joining what Liriel called "this supersecret vampire coven started by a couple in North Carolina. They did these rituals of blood-drinking and held the philosophy that vampires are supposed to live off human beings, and therefore human life is worth nothing. This group attracted the attention of someone who reported them to the FBI."

The experience disturbed Liriel, and she took a brief break from any other VRI activities. Later on, she started up her newsletter again, though on a limited scale. Currently, she says, she has about thirty subscribers.

In recent months, Liriel's professional and personal lives have both taken turns for the better. She has left United Way and is employed full time by King County, where she says her supervisor and co-workers are well aware of her vampire-related newsletter and other activities.

"They accept it like, well, that's part of her personality, and that's the way she is," Liriel said. "I feel glad that they seem to like me and value me."

At one point Liriel, who never formally finished or even started high school, tackled some college courses. She enjoyed physics and thought about becoming a physicist, but she gave up the idea because she thought it would take too long.

Liriel also has a steady boyfriend, one who has stayed around for two and a half years and also has accepted her interest in vampirism, though she says he's "not into vampires at all. His name is Andy, and he's living off an inheritance now. He does teach guitar lessons, though. You know, he was born just two days after me. We're both twenty-four; babies, really."

There's another important change in Liriel's life: She no longer believes real vampires exist, or at least the back-from-the-dead kind she once was convinced had to be around somewhere.

"By this time I've read so many books on fictional vampires that every time I pick up a new one I think, 'Hey, I've read all this before,'" she said. "I know there are people who believe they are vampires and act it out, but a real vampire, somebody who's been dead and comes back with supernatural powers? No, there aren't any. I've come to that conclusion. I'd be mighty surprised if one knocked on my door."

This doesn't mean Liriel plans to shut down the VRI. She remains devoted to finding out why people are mesmerized by the whole vampire legend. As part of her research, she regularly subscribes to other vampire underground publications, always inviting readers to write to the VRI and take part in its surveys. Liriel is suspicious, though, of organizations she thinks may be trying to con gullible young vampire wannabes into spending a lot of money for publications full of gibberish or hokey "vampire" products like rings, medallions, and fake fangs.

Seattle's Temple of the Vampire especially irked her "because I mostly work at cost and stuff like that, and they want a hundred dollars a year just for people to join them at an introductory level."

Liriel thinks she may be "growing out" of her vampire obsession, but that doesn't mean she's ready to go cold turkey.

"Maybe I'll do this for five more years, though now I can see kind of a limit to my research," she said. "I know this vampire craze is still going on, but I think it might climax this year or next year. After that, not so many people will want to be acting like vampires. It's cyclical, you know? Maybe a generation ago there were some people who got that way because they loved that vampire TV series, 'Dark Shadows.' This generation probably got into it because of Anne Rice."

Society does have a variety of real vampire, Liriel thinks, one that feeds off the work of others.

"It's the corporate vampire, if you will," she explained. "Big executives like Bill Gates with Microsoft. He and people like him have so much power, and the power comes from the fact they have people underneath them, the pyramid thing, all these employees making $7.50 an hour, and they're the vampire at the top. They take all these people's time and money and live off it at the top. People feel it, and in a subconscious way they understand that this is the real idea of the vampire, someone who takes while you give. And in families, the parents are under the corporate vampire, and the kids are under all kinds of people—parents, school, their first jobs. So the kids have free time, and they think, 'Maybe I want to be the one who's the vampire.'"

As for Liriel, she'd like to be a writer—and a mother.

"I'm beginning to think about going back to California, maybe to San Luis Obispo," she said. "My mother and sister and I have been talking about moving back to L.A. I might take Andy along. I do know in the future I definitely want to write full time, and I plan on maybe not marriage but certainly children."

Meanwhile, Liriel says she doesn't regret her experiences, either as a pseudovampire or a vampirism researcher.

"Trying vampire life can be good," she concluded. "I've learned a lot from it. It just depends how far you take it. I think I took it just about far enough."

*"My vampire nature has been for me the greatest adventure of my life; all that went before it was confused, clouded... It was only when I became a vampire that I respected for the first time all of life."*

INTERVIEW WITH THE VAMPIRE
ANNE RICE, 1976

# 2

# *The Vampire in Literature*

---

Liriel wasn't the only person who became obsessed with vampirism after reading *Interview With the Vampire*, Anne Rice's best-selling novel that was originally published in 1976. Rice has since written four sequels in what became known as *The Vampire Chronicles*, most of which have also been best-sellers. Many of the vampires we interviewed agreed with Liriel that *Interview With the Vampire* had been a catalyst for their own blood-drinking experiences. Even those who said they felt Rice's characters didn't realistically depict actual vampirism—Orlando's Dark Rose in particular made that criticism—owned some of her books.

Not all real vampires, though, knew Rice was only the latest author whose English-language works influenced today's vast, ever-growing underground vampire culture in America. Rice is actually third in a line of key writers whose seminal fiction ultimately shaped the modern-day image of sophisticated, seductive vampires. The middle author among the three, Bram Stoker, is certainly recognized for writing *Dracula* in 1897. But Dr. John Polidori, the true father of modern-day vampire fiction, was even denied writer's credit when *The Vampyre*, his groundbreaking short story, was published in Britain's *New Monthly Magazine* in

1819. So it's ironic, if not especially surprising, that most of Rice's modern-day glut of fans have no idea it's Polidori they should really thank, since his work inspired Stoker, whose work in turn inspired Rice.

Modern vampire fiction, then, dates back the better part of two hundred years. It began with a European vacation in 1816 that's already famous among sophisticated horror fiction fans, and rightly so. A small group of famous writers left England in the summer months of that year to spend a few weeks abroad in Geneva, Switzerland.

The party included poet Percy Bysshe Shelley, his future wife Mary Godwin, and bad-tempered George Gordon Byron, better known as Lord Byron. Polidori, employed as Byron's personal physician, also came along.

Byron was in a bad mood. He had reason to be. His former lover, Lady Caroline Lamb, had just published a scandalous novel titled *Glenarvon,* and its nasty leading character, Clarence de Ruthven, was clearly a thinly disguised caricature of Byron. As a result, Byron was being mocked on both sides of the English Channel after Lady Caroline's fictional skewering. In the book, de Ruthven even joined forces with Satan, causing unpleasant rumors about Byron's possible affiliation with witchcraft in real life.

On the trip to Geneva, Byron and Polidori quarreled. It probably concerned Byron's drinking and use of the drug laudanum. The weather, apparently, was rotten. Byron was also irritated with the fifth member of the group, Mary's sister Claire, who was pregnant with Byron's child. Probably to calm everyone down, Mary Godwin (later Shelley) suggested group members amuse themselves by each writing a ghost story, though in later years she sometimes said it was Lord Byron who made the suggestion. Whoever came up with the idea, some of them tried it.

The results were mixed. Percy Shelley didn't write anything. Mary Godwin rose to her own (or Byron's) challenge and started the first chapter of an eventual novel about a doctor named Victor who tried to emulate God by bringing life back to a dead body composed of sewn-together parts of corpses. Her book would be called *Frankenstein.*

Polidori tried to weave a tale about a woman who suffered terrible things after peeking through a keyhole and seeing something she shouldn't have. Mary Godwin Shelley later called the story "terrible," and it was forgotten almost immediately.

Byron decided he'd write a story about a vampire.

Vampire stories as a genre weren't anything new; vampiric folklore telling of dead-yet-alive, blood-drinking creatures had been part of the human experience since the dawn of time. This was true of all cultures, from Japan to India to Europe to the Americas. Until that fateful day when Mary Godwin issued her challenge, though, fictional vampires were anything but the dangerously alluring Children of the Night we read about today. Mostly, they were ugly, misshapen monsters who'd lurch from their graves to snatch sheep or cattle or babies, drain their blood, and return to their messy resting places. Sometimes they'd turn themselves into animals, always predatory beasts native to whatever country a particular author lived in: Indian vampires would inhabit tigers. Eastern European vampires sometimes turned themselves into wolves. In any event, prior to the short story that was about to be written in 1816, it's impossible to imagine any readers of vampire fiction yearning to be vampires themselves.

Byron's story fragment wasn't about an ugly monster. He began writing about a seductively sinister vampire who could walk around London or Europe in the form of a gentleman society dandy and not be recognized as a blood-drinking predator until it was too late. Byron himself must have been familiar with the folklore of eastern Europe. He used the term "vampyre," a form of the Slavic "vampir." At least as far as Byron was concerned, though, the story either didn't work or else he became bored with it. He discarded the pages he'd written and turned his attention back to arguing with Polidori, who left soon afterward.

But sometime during the next three years, Polidori took Byron's story fragment and completed it. *New Monthly Magazine* printed *The Vampyre* in 1819, but attributed the work to Lord Byron. Polidori protested, and eventually the story was credited to him. He wound up being paid thirty English pounds for it, roughly $350 in modern U.S. currency.

Byron wasn't amused, and again for good reason. The blood-drinking hero of the story, who ends up betraying a friend and draining the friend's sister, was named Lord Ruthven, a pointed reminder to readers of Lady Caroline Lamb's character assassination of Byron in her earlier book.

But far more important to future generations of vampire-fixated readers was Polidori's depiction of his evil hero. Ruthven was the complete opposite of the gargoyle vampires of previous folklore. He was handsome and charming, though destructively so. Ruthven came back to life after being murdered by thieves. Afterward, he seduced his best friend's sister, and, on their wedding day, drained her of blood as a desperate rescue attempt failed. The sexual implications couldn't be missed, either, and they no doubt were partially responsible for the story becoming a runaway hit.

Byron, stung, eventually did publish what became known as his "fragment," but only after he removed all mention of vampire activity from it. Maybe Byron hoped by doing so he'd end the vampire craze he and Polidori had started, but that didn't happen. Instead, other authors all over England and Europe rushed to get their own vampire stories into print, and in many cases they created vampire leading men in Lord Ruthven's seductive, evil image. Authors whose names are regularly included on high school and college English class reading lists—Dumas, Poe, Gogol, Tolstoy, Swinburne, Hawthorne, Bierce—all tried their hands at a vampire tale or two.

By 1890, there were so many vampire books in print that Bram Stoker, the manager of London's Lyceum Theatre, must have read some of them. Stoker himself had been published a few times. His first works were rather spooky children's fairy tales; he'd also written a novel called *The Snake's Pass*. But his various notes and diaries make it clear that he started his most famous writing project in 1890, and devoted much of the next six years to researching and writing *Dracula*.

Like Polidori, Stoker gave a modern British twist to eastern European vampiric folklore. His main character took the name of a notorious Wallachian family—"Dracul" can mean either "the dragon" or "the devil" in that language. Stoker's Dracula properly hailed from Transylvania and lived in a castle in the Carpathian Mountains. The crumbling ruins of Vlad Tepes's real-life fortified home can still be seen there today. The various Romanian protections against the vampires of their mythology found their way into Stoker's tale—garlic, crucifixes, and so forth. And, in the manner of Lord Ruthven before him, Count Dracula preyed in a blood-drinking yet sensual way on young, virginal English women.

Where Stoker went Polidori one better, though, was by endowing his vampire with even vaster powers. Dracula could transform himself into smoke and waft away. He summoned wolves, crawled down castle walls, and even turned into a bat. Stoker relied on folklore for the wolves, but the idea of vampire-as-bat was entirely his own. Probably he recalled the recent discovery of blood-drinking bats in South America and decided to incorporate that theme into his novel.

It's also true that Stoker's Dracula was physically repulsive. His eyebrows were "massive, almost meeting over the nose." His ears were pointed on top, his breath was "rank," and clumps of hair grew in the centers of his palms. Still, he had a harem of female vampires at his castle, and again Stoker one-upped Polidori by making these female vampires every bit as deadly as their male counterpart, though Dracula clearly ruled them.

Published in 1897, *Dracula* was a sensation. More than a century later, it's still popular. Stoker was frustrated in subsequent attempts to top it. He failed, and of his later books, modern readers might recall only *The Lair of the White Worm*, since it was turned into a very bad movie about fifteen years ago.

*Dracula*, of course, inspired hundreds of movies, many of them awful. But enough classics, both of the popular and cult variety, were created to extend the Dracula/vampire myth through several more generations. And, much like *The Vampyre*, *Dracula* spawned innumerable copycat vampire novels, almost all of which failed to capture the mesmerizing evil of Stoker's book.

Then, seventy-nine years later, came *Interview With the Vampire*.

Anne Rice's vampires were the equal of Stoker's Count, and then some. They possessed awesome powers like Dracula. They slept in coffins, had to avoid sunlight, and fed on the blood of innocent victims. But unlike the cruel Count, who planned to come to England and perpetrate his evil deeds there, Rice's blood-drinkers sometimes suffered through various crises of conscience. Of particular note to modern readers was Lestat, introduced in *Interview With the Vampire* as a vicious predator with little regard for human life and less for human feelings. Gradually, in Rice's sequels, Lestat reached higher moral ground. *The Vampire Lestat*, Rice's second *Vampire Chronicle*, found Lestat forming a rock-and-roll band and telling readers his side of the story. *Queen of the Damned* had Lestat battling an all-powerful female vampire, and, after winning, assuming her powers. *Tale of the Body Thief* offered an unexpected plot twist: For a while, Lestat lost his vampire powers and had to live as a human. Eventually, in *Memnoch the Devil*, Lestat discovered himself being recruited by both God and Satan as a potential second-in-command.

As presented by Rice, Lestat is a predator, but often a caring one. He is also a beautiful, sensual being, though Rice's self-dubbed *Vampire Chronicles* lack the more explicit sex scenes she includes in other books. (When the movie based on *Interview With the Vampire* was released, Tom Cruise played Lestat.) The combination clearly worked. Lestat is worshiped by many of today's real-life vampires. Quite a few think he must actually exist. In one of Liriel's Vampirism Research Institute questionnaires, she asked respondants to vote on the possible existance of "Dracula-type" and "Lestat-type" vampires. Sixty-three percent thought Dracula was strictly fictional. Seventy-two percent believed a "Lestat-type" might really be around somewhere.

Rice set many of Lestat's adventures in her hometown of New Orleans, and fans of her books began making pilgrimages to that fabled Louisiana city, where they'd sightsee and point out all the landmarks and real buildings Rice included in her stories. And every October, New Orleans is the site of a premier event among vampire practitioners and enthusiasts: the Anne Rice's Vampire Lestat Fan Club's Annual Gathering of the Coven Halloween Party.

In the November 1995 issue of *VRI News*, correspondent Cindy Zeuli spent two rapturous pages describing the event. Among other adventures, Zeuli participated in the fan club's "On the Trail of the Vampire" tour of *Vampire Chronicle* sites, including a building said to be Lestat's town house.

"It was cool because we got to meet other fans," Zeuli wrote. "We all got a spider ring and a sticker to wear, and the guide showed us her garlic, cross, and holy water, but said we wouldn't have to worry about vampires anyway because it was daylight. Interestingly enough, nobody in the group wanted to be protected from vampires at all!"

That night, the ball fulfilled Zeuli's wildest expectations. She wore fake fangs, met a cast member of the *Interview* film, and even got a glimpse of Anne Rice herself.

"For a few brief days, I got to step inside Ms. Rice's books and even become a vampire myself for an evening," Zeuli concluded. "We were on the trail of the vampire, and even if we never did catch up with Lestat, at least we were able to follow in his footsteps."

In recent interviews, Rice has said she doesn't anticipate writing another book with Lestat as lead character. Meanwhile, she's become a celebrity herself. During a national book-signing tour to help promote *Memnoch the Devil*, Rice had to hold six-hour signing stints in stores instead of the traditional two-hour signings because her fans turned out in such massive numbers.

It seems impossible that Rice is unaware of her influence on modern-day vampires. We contacted her publisher to request an interview and were told she was away in Europe researching a new book and, therefore, unavailable.

"I guess she has to know some readers believe she isn't just making Lestat up," Liriel mused. "I believed that, but I've changed. I still love her books. I hope she keeps writing them."

Orlando's Dark Rose said she loves Rice's books, too, "but that's where it stops. When I get on America Online on the computer, everybody thinks they know what I'm like because I'm a vampire, and Anne Rice is their whole influence. That's why I started my own publication, *The Dark Rose Journal*, to weed that out. I mean, I'm in one of the vampire chat rooms trying to talk to these people, and they just want to know if I'm like someone in whatever Anne Rice book. I adore Anne Rice, but I don't want to talk about Lestat or those type of characters. They're not like we real vampires are at all. My writing is going to be the anti-Anne Rice, the anti-Lestat."

Yet in the Autumn 1995 edition of *The Dark Rose Journal*, Dark Rose has only good things to say about the film version of *Interview With the Vampire*.

"The various vampires are multidimensional characters who have much more on their minds than just where their next meal is coming from," Dark Rose wrote. "The love-hate relationship between Lestat and Louis is complex and endless, and it would be as compelling if they were, say, Baptists instead of vampires."

The best thing about the film, Dark Rose concluded, was that "the lifestyle of the vampires is not presented as a facet of evil, but rather as an inevitable quirk of nature. Rattlesnakes coil and strike not because they're evil, but because that's what they do. A vampire feeds because it's hungry…"

Besides further refining the Western image of vampires, Rice's other legacy may be inspiring real vampires to write about themselves. Liriel has made several attempts to complete a vampire novel; Dark Rose is working on a nonfiction book, *The Gothic Grimoire*, that, she says, will be published within the next year or so.

For many of Anne Rice's fans, though, the hope will probably remain that maybe, just maybe, her books are based on vampires just as real, if greatly different, than Dark Rose.

"Whether people say so or not, that's what they really want," Liriel said. "They want to believe there's a special super vampire out there."

And until the fourth author emerges to further advance popular perception of fictional vampires as Rice did, and Stoker did, and Polidori did, Lestat will remain, for millions, the epitome of what a real-life vampire must and should be.

*"The theory behind the [vampire] clan is that to sin is to forgive.*
*Forgiveness is salvation, therefore salvation is the ultimate sin. It's kind of a*
*complex thing there."*

GREMLIN

# 3
## Gremlin

We met Gremlin the same night we met Liriel, at a downtown Seattle restaurant named McCormick's on a cold January night. Liriel arrived first and mentioned right away that, though she'd invited Gremlin to join us, she only knew him from a few letters they'd exchanged during the last ten months. He'd read a copy of the VRI News and contacted her.

"He says he's the headmaster of a part of this ancient clan who were among the original vampires," she said. "The letters were interesting. He was trying to explain that his clan was fading out, and he just wanted to tell their story before they were gone."

McCormick's was a fairly upscale place, apparently a watering hole for Seattle yuppies wanting to stop off for a drink or a meal before heading home to the suburbs. Gremlin was late. While we waited for him, a pompous waiter made it clear he wanted us to order food immediately or else leave and let someone else have our table. We stalled, ordering drinks but not dinner, and the waiter huffed around impatiently until Gremlin arrived thirty minutes later. Once he saw Gremlin, the waiter did his best to stay as far away from our table as he could.

In some ways, Gremlin didn't look that threatening or even strange. He was about medium height with a scraggly mustache and beard. Later on, we decided he looked a lot like Christian Slater, the actor. Gremlin's overcoat was battered but clean, and no fangs or other popular vampire accoutrements seemed in evidence—except for the bright green dragon scales tattooed on his left arm and hand. The scales sloped down his wrist and up his fingers, which also had squiggly black tattoos between them. Halfway in the act of handing Gremlin a menu, the supercilious waiter spotted the dragon scales and turned quite pale.

"How much is a cup of coffee?" Gremlin asked him very softly, voice hissing just a little on the S. The waiter seemed to have trouble answering. We told Gremlin not to worry about how much things cost, that dinner was on us. Now that he'd arrived, we all ordered; the waiter shuddered noticeably while we did. Liriel wanted steak. Gremlin asked if he could get a vegetable plate. Nervously, the waiter explained that McCormick's didn't have one, but if the gentleman wanted they could perhaps make up some kind of shrimp dish with a lot of vegetables, and should he go right to the kitchen and ask them to get started on it? He scurried away before Gremlin could answer.

"Pleased to meet all of you," Gremlin muttered in his near-whisper, one word following another with almost painful slowness. Then he leaned back while Liriel did most of the talking. We had the feeling he was checking us out, and we were right. After forty-five minutes, during which time he carefully ate all his shrimp and vegetables, taking tiny bites with his front teeth and then munching delicately, Gremlin started joining in the conversation, saying how glad he was someone wanted to hear his story, how important it would be for someone to write the history of his clan.

"We were, you know, sort of the original vampires," he announced in a much louder voice. Even though the restaurant was crammed with noisy people, Gremlin's voice carried. A man in the next booth leaned so far over toward us that he seemed in danger of falling through a partition onto our table.

For the next thirty minutes, Gremlin dominated the conversation. He kept jumping from one topic to another. It was hard to make sense of what he was saying. Finally, we interrupted to say we wanted to arrange a long interview with him the next day, perhaps late in the afternoon at Liriel's house, where we could set up a tape recorder and be certain not to miss a word.

"If you don't mind, I sort of prefer talking in my own comfort zone," Gremlin said, eyelids at half-mast like a sleepy cat. The lids were so pale that it seemed the pupils of his eyes ought to be gleaming through them. "I have a place on Capitol Hill. I'll give you my number and you can call and come see me after you're done with Liriel."

When we finished the meal—Liriel and Gremlin each had an after-dinner glass of wine, poured by the very nervous waiter for whom we guiltily left a huge tip. We offered rides home, since neither of them had a car and would have to walk or ride the bus. Liriel accepted, but Gremlin smiled and said he preferred walking "out among the people."

On the ride back to her house, Liriel said Gremlin hadn't been what she'd expected.

"I was kind of confused," she admitted. "He talked about being the Headmaster of his clan for thirty years or something. Having done this kind of thing before, invented a fictional story, I felt I recognized it as that. But I don't know. He was different."

The next afternoon we called Gremlin after we'd interviewed Liriel. He told us to come right over and provided very complex directions we could never have followed successfully. Liriel said she thought she knew where his apartment was, though, and volunteered to ride over with us, then take the bus back home.

"Capitol Hill is mostly a fancy area," she said. "A lot of rich kids live there, and there are a lot of gays. I don't think he lives in a rich neighborhood, though. I guess I should tell you there are also a lot of very strange people who hang around that part of town."

This turned out to be true. As we slowly drove down several Capitol Hill streets looking for Gremlin's address, we saw dancing Hare Krishnas, glassy-eyed drug addicts, hookers actively soliciting passersby and innumerable college-age kids all heading in different directions in a big hurry. Storefronts advertised Wiccan books and herbal health foods. Finally the streets turned downright nasty, and Liriel announced we'd arrived at Gremlin's block.

"See you later," she said hastily, obviously trying to get away as quickly as possible. "That's his apartment right there. Nice meeting you. Good luck." She glanced at the dirty tan bricks of Gremlin's two-story apartment complex, with its doors raked by crowbars or claws and lots of windows cracked or missing entirely and replaced with cardboard.

"I hope you guys get out of here alive," Liriel blurted, and spun away down the sidewalk toward the bus stop.

❧

For several minutes, it seemed more a matter of getting in to see Gremlin than getting out alive. The entranceway to the apartment complex was locked, and there was no bell to push. We had his phone number but had no idea where we might find a pay phone. We were about to give up when we heard a tapping at one of the second-floor windows. It was Gremlin. He came outside—there was a second-floor, outdoor walkway leading to a staircase—and opened the door so we could come in.

"You got here," he said in the same soft voice, words once again crawling one after another. "Come upstairs."

Gremlin's apartment was appalling. The walls were filthy with accumulated grease and dirt. There was a stained couch to sit on, and the orange-tan carpet was crusty with spilled food and other things we didn't want to identify. There also were four cats, all immaculately groomed. On a rickety counter separating the living room and kitchen was a cheap CD player; discs by various bands like Nirvana and Metallica were scattered nearby. A bookshelf held a few dozen battered titles, including several Anne Rice paperbacks, and some sort of artwork appeared to be tacked up on a kitchen wall. Crayon scrawlings on yellow paper were taped to the door of the refrigerator. Otherwise, decorations were minimal—a few ragged movie posters, and, on the counter, a framed photo of a very conservatively dressed Gremlin with his arm around a pretty little girl.

"So you came," Gremlin said grandly, still hissing his "S's" and sounding a little surprised. "I want to tell you about my clan. Because of the way they were in the past, and the superstitions that were around in Europe then, they were known as vampires. I'm eager to tell the story."

Gremlin stood behind the counter separating the kitchen from the living room, placing his hands on it and leaning forward in the manner of a preacher lounging behind a pulpit. He was dressed in grubby jeans and a black T-shirt festooned with images of dancing skeletons. Besides the dragon scales on his left forearm and hand, his entire left arm was covered with a gaudy tattoo involving a Grim Reaper and an open grave.

"It all goes back to the time near Genesis," he began. "The clan, which wandered about the Eastern Hemisphere, was known as the Khlysty." He pronounced the word kuh-LIS-tee. "The theory behind the clan is that to sin is to forgive, forgiveness is salvation, therefore salvation is the ultimate sin. It's kind of a complex thing there. Basically, the way we feel is that if you're going to sin, it will be for the sake of the sin or else to hurt people. And we don't believe sinning to hurt people is the best way to go about it."

A few months later, when we met Martin Riccardo, he dismissed Gremlin's Khlysty tale.

"Vampires have always been solitary predators," Riccardo insisted. "If anyone claims there was a group of them working together, well, there's never been any documentation of such a thing."

According to Gremlin, though, the Khlysty vampires traveled through Europe visiting towns and judging the people who lived there. They didn't expect anyone to be perfect. In fact, they explained that sinning was a natural part of life.

"You can't go through life saying, 'Thou shalt not kill,' and then walk across the street and crush a thousand ants," Gremlin lectured. "You can't go through life saying, 'I shall not covet,' because next you'll see someone else's coat and think, 'Boy, that sure would look good on me.' Who are you trying to fool? There's just no way to do it. And a lot of the people ignored their message, but a few said they were making sense and started following them."

Gremlin said the Khlysty had superhuman powers, though he was vague in describing them. He did say the group included an Assassin's Guild to punish anyone carrying sin too far, and that members now preferred to be called "dark souls" instead of "vampires."

"The vampire thing, well, most of the time when people call themselves that, what you've really got is kids in capes." Gremlin sniffed disdainfully. "Go to any Denny's on a Friday night, and you'll see them there. The vampires they believe in are mythological creatures. What we, the Khlysty are, well, everyone is born into this world with a soul. Some are malicious souls; they're born with hate. We in Khlysty have dark souls, like you took a soul and ran it over the coals a little bit. If we have to get attention we can still use the word 'vampire,' because if you say, 'Hi, I'm a dark soul,' that's not gonna turn anyone on or anything."

Gremlin had a tendency to ramble. Trying to keep him focused, we asked how he'd discovered he was a Khlysty member.

"Well, I'm twenty-one now, and this fall I went down to California for a while," he said. "I had a friend who wanted to introduce me to these people he'd met. I introduced myself, and they said they'd wanted to meet me because we'd spoken before. A lot of the things they told me then were things I'd felt throughout my life, and I suddenly understood I was part of this clan, this lifestyle."

Previously, Gremlin hadn't thought much about family origins. He said he'd been raised in Seattle by a single mother. His father was in and out of prisons, though for what crimes Gremlin wasn't quite sure. Gremlin had an older brother and sister, both of whom, he said with obvious contempt, were "pretty normal." Gremlin himself was normal up through eighth grade. His grades were good, and he stayed out of trouble. But during eighth grade Gremlin rebelled. He ended up not finishing school and getting married at seventeen to a girl a year younger.

"I didn't really click with the high school thing," he said.

The marriage lasted three years and produced a daughter, Alexandra, the little girl with Gremlin in the photograph. He beamed when he talked about her.

"I've raised her with the help of her mother," he bragged. "Alex is a loving person. And she knows people. She can tell good ones from bad ones. She lives with her mother, but I have her over here a lot of the time. I've got some of her drawings on my refrigerator. My wife thought I didn't know how to deal with reality, and she divorced me. But with the Khlysty, now things are all right."

Gremlin said his California encounter included a Khylsty "Headmaster" or teacher.

"Each Headmaster is in charge of a certain area and all the other clan members in it," he said. "He told me he has fourteen in his part. I'm now Headmaster of ten or twelve in the upper Northwest. They're in contact every once in a while, usually through the mail."

Once he knew other members of the Khylsty clan, Gremlin said, he began to experience fleeting visions of past lives and times. That led him to believe in reincarnation. Then, too, there were newly acquired powers.

"Afterward, I felt things other people didn't feel, saw things other people didn't see. I've actually been able to tell people the future," he said.

What he didn't do was drink blood. That, Gremlin insisted, was not the way of real vampires or dark souls, only what pretenders did.

"Oh, I've tasted blood now, and it's rather nasty, actually. It's kind of dull," he said. "People who are really like me, well, we live in a rather dark realm. Now I see people walking down the streets, the kids in capes, and they say they're going to suck your blood. Well, if that's what makes a vampire, then I'm not the real thing, because I'm not thirsting for blood. We real ones, what we do, is feed from a soul."

True Dark Souls, the real vampires, Gremlin said, did need to feed off humans. But it was possible to do it in a positive way, to drain the energy needed without in any way hurting the donor.

"It has to do with sex, whether you're homosexual, bisexual, or straight," Gremlin lectured. "Whenever your mate reaches that final point of orgasm, that's a force and power nothing man-made has ever been able to duplicate. We Khlysty just need to touch them at that moment and concentrate on that power, and not really drain it all from them, because you don't want to ruin their time. All you need is a taste." He stretched out a bony arm, index finger extended, and pretended to delicately touch an invisible lover. "See? That's all you need, and that's sufficed me for the past four months."

Uriel, a self-styled "vampyre" who would only contact us in writing, supported Gremlin's description of vampiric psychic feeding involving sex. Her letter read in part, "There are psychic vampires that feed off of psychic energy and vitality but not necessarily blood...Physically, they are often very powerful, and they have great skill in channeling energy, whether to harm or to heal. I term these beings vampyres and consider myself one of them."

Psychic feeding, Uriel wrote later in the February 1996 issue of The International Society of Vampires newsletter, *The Midnight Sun*, allowed the psychic vampire to give great sexual pleasure to his or her partner.

"Though many of my partners have not had the opportunity to compare notes, still they all describe their experience in the same way," she wrote. "It is like riding a single, prolonged orgasm which never dips below ecstacy, but which ebbs and flows in intensity. Even though I am very careful with my partners and endeavor not to take more than they can safely give, still they will often urge me to continue until they have literally passed out beneath me."

In her letter to us, Uriel also predicted any true psychic vampires we encountered would find themselves "immortal in the sense that they are old souls, endlessly reincarnated down the centuries, but gifted—or cursed—with the ability to retain their memories and knowledge of previous lives."

Michelle Belanger, non-blood-drinking publisher of *The Midnight Sun* and several other vampire-related magazines and periodicals, said because of testimony like Gremlin's and Uriel's, "I can acknowledge the possibility of psychic vampires. Some of them are just too sincere and too creative, really. What they describe independently of each other is nothing you'd have found in a book. The stories of psychic vampirism I heard jibe even though the people communicating them are flung all over the world."

And the Khlysty and others of a true vampiric nature, whether blood-drinking or energy-absorbing, are never dangerous to other humans, Gremlin insisted. Pretend monsters, humans who deluded themselves into thinking they were creatures with special powers, are the dangerous ones.

"I've met people who think they're vampires," he droned. "I've met people who think they're werewolves. I've met people who think they're ghosts reincarnated in the flesh. I truly believe they're completely delusional. A lot of the time they've done too many drugs, or they're just kind of lost. They don't really know where they fit in."

Gremlin paused to turn on the heat under a coffeepot. When the coffee was ready, he poured himself a cup but didn't offer us any. This was typical. Most of the time when we interviewed vampires in their homes, whenever they got themselves snacks or drinks they didn't ask if we wanted anything. Dark Rose in Orlando was an exception, as was Martin Riccardo in Chicago. But then Riccardo isn't a vampire himself, just a friend to many of them.

Maybe the caffeine kicked in on Gremlin. After he finished his coffee, he acted much more agitated. For the first time, his words tumbled out in a rush. The change in him was ominous.

Looking down at my feet, I noticed the carpeting in front of the living room window was worn in a straight, narrow line, as though he spent much of his time pacing frantically back and forth, watching people on the street below.

"Why are people so fascinated with vampires?" we asked, mostly to calm him down. But the question had the opposite effect.

"People want to believe there are vampires out there," Gremlin said angrily. "Not just for the romance of it, but because they're tired of dealing with everything bad that happens, like war or pestilence. They want something that's bad, yeah, but still has a tingly side to it. They get that sliver of hope that hey, maybe he'll come over and bite me, and we'll have a little romance or some excitement. Well, sometimes I take their energy without meaning to. I'm sitting across from someone who's just had a quad shot of espresso and still, a minute later, they're yawning and starting to fall asleep."

Gremlin paused, then confessed he was suffering through a tough personal time.

"I'm going through this down period, a lag time, where nothing really interests me," he said. "All the clan Headmasters do this sometimes. I'm not interested in sex or getting energy from someone. I haven't had my daughter over here because it just isn't the right atmosphere right now. I don't know why my ex-wife says I live in a fantasy world. I deal with life in a very realistic way. I have bills. I have a business in the making. I live a very normal life. I wake up, I go to sleep, I work."

Gremlin calmed down momentarily when we asked just what business he had in the making.

"Tattoos," he said proudly. He flipped on a light switch and illuminated the drawings tacked up on the kitchen wall. "These are all my designs. I created them all myself."

Most of the designs seemed ordinary—a few topless women glancing coyly back over their bare shoulders, some writhing snakes, a few hearts and stars and flowers. But several were startling in their savagery—devils grimacing, bloody-eyed monsters leering.

"I did the tattoos on my body myself," Gremlin added. "I always thought it would be neat to have lizard skin. The one on my left arm is very important. It illustrates the experience of my becoming Gremlin. I dreamed it all, you see, death and this gremlin popping up out of the grave. I'm working on another one on my right arm. See, it's drawn already in ink. This is Lucifer, the fallen angel, or any one of the other fallen angels. That has a lot to do with how I view myself and the Khlysty. 'Dark Angel' really connects to describe us."

Gremlin said he hoped to open his own tattoo shop, one that would become famous for Khlysty-inspired designs.

"I'll always continue to be a questioner," he added. "That's why I'm in touch with the Temple of the Vampire. They seem a little adamant in the way they run things. They sent me this brochure that said if I buy this book, buy this ring, and buy this pendant, I'm an active member. In the book, they tell you certain things you have to do to get a higher rank. I haven't bought the book yet. I think it's twenty-five dollars, but I plan on it just to see what they're about. I'm a Khlysty. I'm a truth finder, and if they're not what I'm looking for, I'll know, and then I'm not going to deal with them."

Gremlin then launched into another detailed description of the Khlysty and their activities.

"They called us vampires because we came into towns dressed in dark cloaks," he ranted. "Anyone who said he did not sin was lying. So they would torture these people to actually admit to their sins, and, once they did, the sins were forgiven. I hold no pity toward hardly anyone. I help people because in a direct, hard way, I teach them what they need to know."

In a last attempt to calm Gremlin, we asked why, if he disdained nonclan members claiming to be vampires, he had still written to Liriel and her Vampirism Research Institute.

"I told you I'm a questioner, a seeker of the truth," Gremlin answered. "I sent a letter to Liriel, the same letter I sent to the Temple of the Vampire here in Seattle, because I know the word 'vampire' gets used in a very generic sense. I want to know more. I'm sort of putting ads out seeking dark souls. I'm a collector of souls. Liriel responded and we wrote back, corresponded. The Temple just wanted me to send money."

Gremlin acknowledged many people would think he had made up the whole Khlysty tale.

"Yeah, I can understand where people would say I was living in a fantasy world, and I'd had these problems in the past, no father and didn't graduate high school and all this and that, and now I'm searching for something new," he mumbled. "Actually, I'm living a very good lifestyle. I work at a professional job. I make ten dollars an hour at a psychic line. I used to work for a psychic reading tarot cards. Now I'm working for the psychic line as a bulk mail distributor. I'm putting out the magazine they're going to put on the Internet."

Meanwhile, Gremlin said, the danger remained that the Khlysty could die out. There were enemies, he suggested, who wanted them eliminated. Still, he didn't mind anyone knowing his address in Seattle.

"If they want to come over here, there's not much of a chance they're going to get in," he said, beginning to pace again. "I have security. I have a sword in back. It's under my bed. It's safer than a gun, especially if you have a daughter."

We edged toward the door.

"The Khlysty will stay strong," Gremlin said by way of goodbye. "I have visions, not all the time, but I have visions of dusty roads in Europe. I have dreams of walking through tombs in Egypt and talking to these pharaohs. A lot of it I feel I was there for."

So Uriel had been right.

We hurried out, down the staircase and onto the street. Before getting into the car, we looked back at Gremlin's second-story window. He was pacing directly behind it, and two of the cats were preening themselves on the sill.

# 4
# *The Vampire Marketplace*

Early in our research process, it became apparent that, besides pursuing their own activities in or research about vampirism, many of the people we met were trying to turn a dollar from their blood-drinking or vampire-obsessed brethren. Gremlin wanted to support himself with a tattoo parlor specializing in vampire-related designs. Liriel tried producing and selling *VAMPS* magazine in 1990 to make money, and still charged six dollars for annual subscriptions to her *VRI News*, though she said she only charged enough to break even.

Later on, there was Dark Rose in Orlando. Charter subscriptions to her racy *Dark Rose Journal* cost twenty-six dollars, and she plans to open a Dark Rose 900 Line, too. Eventually, she hopes her *Journal* will evolve into a glossy popular magazine available at most newsstands. Meanwhile, there's her in-progress book, *The Dark Rose Grimoire*, that takes up a lot of her time.

Martin Riccardo of Chicago's Vampire Studies has written three books, two of which concern vampires. He says his third vampirism-related book, *Liquid Dreams of Vampires*, will be published in October 1996. In it, he will examine how vampire themes occupy so many people's sleeping visions, and what exactly that may mean.

Vlad, founder of Chicago's The Dark Theater, spent years as a frustrated rock and roller trying to get the public to listen to his music. A student of music history who lists Jimi Hendrix, the Artist Formerly Known as Prince, and Franz Liszt as his idols, Vlad laughed when he openly called himself "a whore, you bet. I'm a blood-drinker anyway, and a few years ago I was talking to my agent about what would really get my music out in front of people, and I thought about fangs. I went to a cosmetologist and had 'em made. So now we put on a vampire show. I say that when people come, if they just look at the fangs, then I don't want them there, but I don't mind if it's the fangs or vampire image that gets them there in the first place." Using The Dark Theater as a springboard, Vlad has organized and hosted two "Vampire Circus" events that drew thousands of blood-drinkers and vampire fans from all over the world.

In Cleveland, nonvampires Michelle and David Belanger founded Shadowfox Publications after their lifelong fascination with vampirism resulted in contact with sufficient blood-drinkers and other vampire fans to convince them there was a large, untapped market for vampire-related printed material. Their *Publication Information 1995* listed several magazines and newsletters. These included *The Midnight Sun*, the Official Newsletter of the International Society of Vampires (subscriptions are thirteen dollars in the U.S., fourteen dollars in Canada, fifteen dollars overseas); a combination subscription to *The Midnight Sun* and "our elegant quarterly of poetry and fiction," *Shadowdance* (thirty dollars in the U.S., thirty-three dollars in Canada, thirty-five dollars overseas); and *Voices in the Shadows*, described as featuring "the work of many of the best new voices in the (vampire) genre today...crisply laid out in a digest-sized format with a cardstock cover and featuring an affordable cover price of five dollars U.S., six dollars Canada and seven dollars overseas." Also listed were two developmental Shadowfox projects—The Lost Souls Vampire Live Action Troup, which would help organize and run "live action games," and the *Dark Moon Series*, a collection of successively issued books "on occult topics such as vampirism, magic, necromancy, and shamanism."

Martin Riccardo told us about Vampires of America, based in Wichita, Kansas. VOA offered *Vampire Theatre: A Vampire Videozine*. In part, the ad copy for *Vampire Theatre* urged: "If you're a vampire or just a vampire lover, grab your video camera and start taping your stories, mini-movies, or do your own vampire interviews. But tell and show all you want! And send them to us!"

In smaller type, the ad noted, "This videozine specializes in vampires and is not rated."

No mention of payment for accepted submissions was made on the flyer we saw. Contributors apparently are rewarded only with seeing their videos presented as part of a greater "videozine" whole. A four-issue subscription costs forty dollars, with thirty seconds of video commercial space going for fifty dollars.

Martin Riccardo was both a subscriber and contributor. He played us the latest *Vampire Theatre* videozine. Its featured video was the first segment of what was billed as an ongoing vampire serial. It involved a group of young performers pretending to be vampires catching a female victim in an alley and bringing her into a park so they could feed on her. The installment ended just before they did so. There was no nudity or graphic violence. A lot of the segment was badly lit and somewhat out of focus.

"It's just a fun thing," Riccardo said. "I give them some material of me interviewing writers of vampire novels, for instance. This video thing is just another way for people interested in vampirism to communicate back and forth."

Every vampire we interviewed seemed to subscribe to several undergound newsletters. Each issue of these would include advertisements for other newsletters or vampire-related products. The Autumn 1995 *Dark Rose Journal* included sales pitches from Brian

Demski of Hollywood, California, for "custom skull and skeletal furniture, candelabra, movie props, and merchandise." Those interested were requested to send four dollars for more information. Nosferatu Productions, also of Hollywood, simply wanted a stamped, self-addressed envelope for a 1995 catalog of "one-stop vampire shopping," featuring "music, videos, jewelry, cosmetics, posters, T-shirts, and much more." Someone from Portland, Oregon, who identified himself as "Scary," even ran a personals ad seeking "a petite, intelligent, feminine catwoman for the creation of cambion demon-spawn and musical-artistic conspiracy." To help such catwomen decide if they cared to respond, Scary listed his own interests as "leather (mmmmm), Satanism, military history, vampire lore, and tantric indulgences." Dark Rose said she charged ten cents a word for these "unclassified" ads. Subscribers to her journal could place brief ads for free.

Often, though, vampire underground journals and newsletters ran advertisements that seemed to boost competing publications; sometimes they didn't even charge for these. *The Midnight Sun's* January 1996 issue, for instance, featured a large back-page ad labeled "Other Organizations of Interest," listing eleven organizations or publications, including *The Dark Rose Journal*. The February issue expanded the listing to thirteen publications, with *The Dark Rose Journal* featured again along with Liriel's Vampirism Research Institute.

"We all help each other," Michelle Belanger said simply. "We're all developing ideas as we go along. We want to be easily accessible to anyone who's interested."

That didn't prove to be entirely true of one of the best-known sources for vampire-related information and products. Most vampires we interviewed made at least occasional reference to Temple of the Vampire, which listed as its address a post office box in the Seattle suburb of Lacey.

The Temple is, in all respects, an enigmatic sort of organization. It publishes a newsletter called *Lifeforce* for its members, as well as an advanced series of publications including *The Vampire Predator Bible*, *The Vampire Priesthood Bible*, *The Vampire Sorcery Bible*, and *The Vampire Adept Bible*. A Temple information sheet sent to prospective members begins, "Yes, Vampires do exist. Thank you for your interest in the Temple," and goes on to list various levels of membership along with the flat claim, "We are the Masters of the World."

Both Liriel and Dark Rose gave us some Temple materials. Neither was pleased with the organization. Dark Rose said she had briefly corresponded with a Temple official in an attempt to write a story about the group in her *Dark Rose Journal.*

"I read their stuff, and it was obvious whoever was writing it knew a lot of history," she said. "So when I first wrote them and said I wanted some information, they said fine, but then added, like a warning, 'We're watching you!' which I thought was pretty strange. Then I wrote back asking how they obtained access to supposedly hidden vampire teachings, and why, if they're a select society like they claim, they take anybody as members. I never heard back."

Liriel's complaint was the Temple's emphasis on money—specifically, how much of it their members should send them and for what.

"I'm going to see if a friend wants to join me in conducting a covert investigation," she promised. "They always want more money for one thing, then another. It definitely offends my sense of fairness."

We wanted to do some investigating ourselves while we were in Seattle, but it wasn't possible. The P.O. box was no starting point; post office officials won't disclose who rents them. Dark Rose had a fax number for the Temple, but when we tried to use it the number was no longer in service. The Lacey Chamber of Commerce had no record of the Temple.

The Seattle newspapers didn't have any information about the group in their files. A last-ditch call to the Lacey Police Department didn't turn up anything, either.

But someone was running the Temple, and it was obviously someone intelligent. The various Temple newsletters and publications were well-written, and the information included would gladden the heart of any prospective vampire. Sharp business instincts were in evidence, too. Nearly every page of every publication noted the contents were copyrighted by Temple of the Vampire.

Some of the Temple's materials are scary and deliberately so. The group's four-page information sheet notes early on that "Vampires are the predators of humans," and continues, "We are the few who truly rule this material world, and those who throw their lot with us are wise indeed...Ours is a selfish and brutal philosophy dedicated to personal survival and triumph. We have no interest in humanity as a whole other than in how they may serve us." The information sheet goes on to claim that ancient vampires "created Christianity, Buddhism, Hinduism, Islam, and all other major world religions to produce docility and compliance with the Rule of the Masters"—vampires, naturally.

Especially to confused kids, that could seem to be impressive stuff. But almost as much space in the newsletters is spent hawking memberships and Temple products as is used to reveal complex vampire chants and ceremonies.

"Lifetime memberships" are granted "for a donation of money or some other valuable commodity of exchange." Lifetime members can't pursue "advanced study and elevation" within the group, but they are permitted to buy *The Vampire Bible* (twenty-five dollars), ring (forty-nine dollars), or medallion (thirty-nine dollars). Active memberships are pricier—one hundred dollars annually or monthly dues of ten dollars after paying a twenty dollar initiation fee. Rejected applications, the newsletter promised, would be accompanied by full refunds, but we never met anyone who had applied and not been accepted.

Those "selected" as active members are then required to turn in monthly activity reports, responding to such questions as: "How many Temple advertisements or cards have you distributed this month?" And, "How many persons have you contacted for membership this month?"

"It's like a vampire pyramid scheme," scoffed Victoria, a Chicago vampire.

Still, the information sheet's final admonition to prospective members is a brutally effective one, roughly equivalent to the hard-sell pitch familiar to anyone who has ever shopped for a used car—buy now or regret it forever.

The warning reads, "Vampirism is real and most ancient. Mortal life is swift and short. We may pick and choose amongst the billions to replenish the elite. You have just this one opportunity for life undying. Your next actions will decide your future as either just another mortal lost to the winds of time, or as one who will truly join Us to become a Vampire, an undying Ruler of this earth."

Temple newsletters shilling products combine persuasion with unsubtle threats. The "within lies fact and fancy" disclaimer notwithstanding, the newsletters make it clear correspondents could question or anger Temple leaders only at great personal risk.

One 1994 issue includes a letter noting, "While your magazine is truly entertaining, I could not help but notice your assortment of self-contradictions," with the writer adding a nine-point list of suggestions and corrections to earlier newsletter statements.

In an accompanying response, the Temple notes: "We have published the above letter as a sampling of some of the nonsense this office wades through from humans with delusions of grandeur…This Temple disclaims any responsibility for the writer's recent death…The writer sent this letter unsigned, assuming this would shield his identity. The Temple sends its condolences to his survivors." The Lacey Police Department has no record of a murder investigation involving the Temple. Therefore, this appears to be fancy rather than fact.

Not everyone we interviewed considered the Temple an out-and-out scam. Martin Riccardo thought the Temple "has a lot of people comfortable and happy being part of the organization. It's a vampire form of the Rosicrucians. They do not drink blood in any form—not people blood, not animal blood. For some people who want to get into the world of vampires, that can be a very positive thing, because it eliminates a lot of dangers just from disease or AIDS alone."

If the Temple is, in fact, run out of a home or storefront, Riccardo said, "most pagans and other alternative religions will meet in people's homes because they don't have any official church buildings. I do not agree with all their precepts and philosophy. They have come out with very good, interesting publications. I have every intention of staying on good terms with them."

Riccardo added that he thought the Temple had actually held a "conclave" in Seattle sometime in 1995, though none of the Seattle vampires we met said they'd heard anything about it, including Liriel and Gremlin, who'd bought some of the Temple products.

Riccardo liked *Bloodlines* enough to send the Temple an enthusiastic letter of endorsement, which was reprinted in a subsequent issue. Riccardo praised the periodical "as certainly one of the best, far above most of the schlock in the public arena. It seems you have a highly intelligent membership."

Dark Rose had bought the Temple's *Vampire Bible* for twenty-five dollars, and she showed it to us. It consisted of twenty-four 8½-by-11-inch pages, plus a cover of slightly thicker paper.

Again, the "fact and fancy" disclaimer appeared above a table of contents that included "The Vampire Creed," "The Dragon Speaks," "The Calling of the Undead Gods," "The Secret Methods of Vampirism," "The Predator of Humans," "The Book of Dreaming," and "The Coming Apocalypse." Printed in hard-to-read gothic script, the various chapters demonstrated an elegant writing style. And, amid exhortations to realize humans lived to be dominated by vampires, there were occasional comforting hints that the Temple didn't endorse or even condone violence. One sentence in "The Predator of Humans" chapter even warned, "The murder or harming of any human being or other animal will result in immediate and permanent expulsion from the Temple." Of course, this rule was not entirely selfless. Killing humans, the unidentified writer noted, simply reduced the vampire supply of food: "We need humans as much as humans need crops and cattle."

Temple-printed materials also emphasized that truly evolved vampires don't drink blood anyway. Instead, they learn to draw "life essence" from humans. Gremlin had said this was the way of the Khlysty, too, and Dark Rose said she nourished herself with "lifeforce" far more often than with blood.

Over dinner one night in Chicago, Vlad paused between bites of pizza to say he found nothing wrong with individual blood-drinkers or vampire organizations trying to sell vampirism-related newsletters or other products.

"The ideal is to make your living doing something you enjoy, or being involved with something you enjoy," he said. "Yeah, there have to be a lot of scam outfits jerking people around. 'Buy our crap, be a real vampire.' But otherwise, hey, have fun and get what you can out of it. Give people what they want and get their money for doing it. Blood-drinkers have bills to pay, too, you know?"

*"I am a vampyre. There's vampyre and vampire—vampire is the Hollywood side of it. . .I want to dispel the old Hollywood notions. We're going to work one person at a time."*

VICTORIA

# 5
## *Victoria*

Chicago provided an especially bitter winter afternoon when we went to interview Victoria. The official temperature hovered around ten degrees, the windchill was too ridiculous even to think about, and snow flurries coated over the car windshield faster than frantically swiping wipers could clear the glass.

The chore of driving to Victoria's apartment was made even more difficult by her absolute inability to offer directions. She worked selling lingerie and jewelry for a well-known retailer. The store was in a large mall in a Southwest Chicago suburb. Victoria could tell us how to find her place from the mall—problem was, she wasn't at all certain how to get from our hotel to the mall, even though she'd been living in Chicago for more than a year.

The night before, we'd met Victoria for dinner so we could get acquainted under informal circumstances. Though the restaurant where we met was centrally located, she'd still gotten horribly lost, ending up a good thirty miles away, halfway around the other side of Chicago. When Victoria did arrive, she had her boyfriend in tow—a twenty-four-year-old named Malcolm who sported a green Mohawk haircut and wore more jewelry in his nose than most women adorn themselves with during their entire lives. His fingernails were painted blue.

But Malcolm paled in comparison to Victoria. Short and a bit overweight, decked out in a bright red dress, thirty-year-old Victoria had long, limp brown hair and a rather high-pitched, squeaky voice. She wore clunky glasses with heavy black plastic frames and quarter-inch-thick lenses. If the old-fashioned cat's-eye frames were still around, it seemed certain Victoria would have been wearing them. She giggled constantly, and usually talked with her hand or at least one or two fingers pressed against her mouth. In all, she was perfectly reminiscent of the aunt or distant cousin at family reunions who sits in a corner and causes all the other relatives to roll their eyes and say, "Well, she's really a very sweet person."

In other words, if Victoria is a vampire, anybody could turn out to be.

And she is. According to Victoria, her aim in life is to "break down the stereotypes" that keep people from accepting vampyres—the spelling is important, she insisted—as normal human beings who just like to drink blood now and then.

"It's sad what people think of us," she said when we finally found her apartment. "When people don't understand something, they automatically decide it's bad."

Victoria had dressed up for the interview. She wore a patterned silk blouse, a long, black, ankle-length dress, and pea green socks. The apartment was decorated with framed horror movie posters— *The Crow*, *Wes Craven's New Nightmare*—and a poster from the Showtime cable TV series *The Red Shoe Diaries*. Rickety bookshelves were crammed with a few hardcover titles and a lot of paperbacks, novels by Stephen King and Anne Rice and Dean Koontz as well as nonfiction like *The Good Witch*, *The Living Witch*, and *Urban Pagan*. There were some movies on videocassette, too—*Forrest Gump*, *Dances With Wolves*, and the Frances Ford Coppola version of *Dracula*.

Interspersed on the walls between the posters were autographed photos of heavy metal rock bands, including Poison,

Deliverance, Firehouse, and Demon. Most of the autographs were personalized to Victoria. It seemed a bit odd that such a shy, frumpy young woman would have made the acquaintance of famous rock and rollers.

"Oh, I've worked as a volunteer public relations agent with rock bands since I was fourteen," Victoria explained. "I wanted to get out and do some of the things other kids were doing because I'd been brought up in a very sheltered home. So at concerts my friends and I would sneak backstage and hang out with the bands. This was in the early '80s when concert security was real lenient. We'd run to the store for the bands and get M&Ms or cigarettes or whatever they needed. I hung out with Poison for a while, and it surprised me when I snuck backstage at a Warrant show, and the lead singer shouted my name and gave me a big hug. He'd heard of who I was."

As Victoria chatted, her two black cats wandered across her lap and jumped from chair to sofa to chair. Malcolm lounged on the couch, staring trancelike at the television where a documentary on insects was being broadcast. Victoria sat next to him, absentmindedly patting his thigh or stroking the cats whenever they came within reach. It was a disarmingly domestic scene.

Her childhood, Victoria noted, included a lot of moving around the country.

"I was born in Pasadena, Texas," she said, the words muffled a bit because her hand was over her mouth. "My father's in the oil business, and my mother's been a housewife for eternity, I believe. Usually, we moved every three to five years."

As a little girl, Victoria wanted to be a singer. In one house where her family lived, she said, there was a raised fireplace with a screen in front of it that could be opened by cords. Victoria would climb up on the fireplace, pretending it was a stage, and sing into the screen's cords as though they were microphones.

"In school, I'd learn the subjects but suck on the tests," she confessed. "I tried college, lots of them, Oklahoma State, art college, and then American Airlines academy. I wanted to be a gate agent, a ticket agent, anything but a pilot or a mechanic."

Victoria didn't end up with a job at American. She scored a 97 on her final preemployment exam, and the airline required 99 or 100.

"I ended up working retail after that," she said. "I've been doing it most of my life."

Two lifelong interests, though, dominated Victoria's off-duty hours. She loved music, and played keyboards. Sometimes she was part of short-lived bands, finding new ones to join every place that her family moved, most often in Texas or Oklahoma.

Then there was the occult.

"That began as a childhood interest," Victoria said. "Things like that always intrigued me. I'm into Wicca and the whole Gothic vampire thing, and have been since I was fifteen or sixteen. Wicca is earth magic, mind over matter, understanding the world around you and yourself internally. I studied Wicca with two or three different people, and also I just have this sense of things."

Even in Texas and Oklahoma, Victoria said, she found other people who were interested in Wicca and the occult. Some of the friends she made were students of vampirism as well.

"It was something lots of people talked about," she recalled. "We read the Anne Rice books, we saw the movies, we were open to accepting whatever it had to offer."

Butch, a boyfriend in Fort Worth, introduced Victoria to actual vampirism.

"I was in my early twenties, and this guy and I were living together," she said. "He liked to turn blood-drinking into a ceremony. He was involved in both black and white magic, so he used blood a lot in spell casting. And blood-drinking was involved in sex, too. That's how I first did it."

Victoria discovered she liked drinking blood. Eventually, liking turned into craving, though not as a constant thing.

"Some mornings since then I just wake up craving blood like you might wake up craving milk or chocolate or carbohydrates or whatever," she said in her little-girl voice. "Having to have human blood is just a personal trait. At first I did it just with my boyfriend. It was the two of us, and later on it was with us and two other people."

Usually, Victoria said, she would use pins to prick donors for blood. She never took very much. She also allowed her donors to drink her blood, "but just a few drops. Whether I'm drinking blood or donating it, either way for me is an intense high. I don't know exactly how to describe it. I guess it's euphoric. And after the intensity from drinking the blood subsides, for a long time afterward I feel settled."

Victoria's testimony matched a description of occasional blood-drinkers we'd heard earlier from Martin Riccardo.

"After the first few experiences, they begin to crave blood, though they usually just take small amounts," Riccardo said. "People get the idea of all kinds of blood flowing all over the place. It's almost never that way. Sometimes they'll use a sterilized pin and make a pinprick in the skin, or sometimes they'll make a small cut for what some of them call 'sipping blood.' It is important to them to feed their craving, but they are not psychotics or criminals. They will always get voluntary donors."

Victoria agreed. While she had her first blood-drinking during sex, she explained, she would never make a lover let her have some of his blood if he felt uncomfortable with the idea.

"I don't have to drink someone's blood to have a relationship with him," Victoria said. "Malcolm and I don't do that."

Without taking his eyes from the TV, Malcolm muttered, "Blood-drinking doesn't interest me. The dark undertones of it are what I'm more interested in." He didn't elaborate.

After she began drinking blood, Victoria said, she decided she was a vampyre, with the word spelled in the old-fashioned eastern European way. By her definition, a vampyre is a blood-drinker who doesn't claim any supernatural powers or expect to live forever.

"Those other superstitions are just made up," Victoria scoffed. "The movies create a silly image. I remember once when my friends and I were leaving a movie in Fort Worth, this vampyre movie, and we were all Gothed out in the black and with the white ruffles and everything. A little girl came up to us and asked, 'Are you really vampyres?' And we believed in telling the truth, so we said we were. Then she asked, 'Can you really fly?' Before I could answer, one guy in our group goes, 'If we could fly, do you think we'd still be in this lousy town?' But I made sure to tell her no, we couldn't fly, and that we didn't hurt people to get their blood or anything like that. Maybe she went away thinking vampyres were good after all. I hope so."

Victoria eventually broke up with her Fort Worth boyfriend. She moved to Seattle because she wanted to live near mountains, and she thought she might be able to get a job in the travel industry there.

"After Texas and Oklahoma, Seattle was a nice change," she said. "People there are open and friendly, they let you be who-ever you are. When I got to Seattle, I basically hid all my ankhs and stuff, which is what I did anytime I moved someplace new, especially in Oklahoma. But in Seattle people would just come up to me and say, 'Are you a witch?' I'd say, 'Yeah,' and they'd say, 'Cool,' and that was it."

Not everything went well for Victoria in Seattle. She met a man and got married, but the marriage didn't work out. It wasn't because of her blood-drinking or interest in Wicca, she said.

"Mostly, when I tell people about being a vampyre, they understand," Victoria noted. "Of course, I've gotten various reactions. One friend of mine, when I told her, jumped back and said, 'You're not going to bite me, are you?' Really, she did that. And I had to explain that vampyres do not go around indiscriminately biting people. Then there's the other extreme, a guy named Eric. I think he sensed what I was. He was kind of spooling me along with all these mind games, like we'd go see vampyre movies and he'd ask, 'What do you feel about this?' Anyway, I finally told him I was a vampyre, and he said, 'Cool, I knew you were. I was just waiting for you to tell me.'

Victoria and her husband divorced after being married just eighteen months.

"He took all the money, so I had to move back in with my parents," she said ruefully. "My father hired me to work for this computer company he had going. Eventually, he decided to bring it to Chicago, and that's how I got here, though I work for a store in the mall now. Chicago's all right, but I really miss Seattle."

Victoria devotes much of her time away from work to corresponding with other vampirism enthusiasts and trying to help change the vampire's general bad-guy image.

"When I heard Rosemary Guiley was writing her book, I got in touch with her to try to help dispel the stereotype of the evil vampyre," Victoria said. "I've been writing to Martin Riccardo at Vampire Studies for more than a year. He knows a lot about everything. I'd been hearing Vlad's name and his music for about ten years, but I only got to meet him last night. I like to talk to people like him, like Martin Riccardo, or communicate with people like that one-on-one. I'm not a subscriber to any of the vampyre journals. I don't like covenism or joining groups."

Victoria said she's bothered by the way books and movies create a false image of vampire lifestyles and longevity.

"Real vampyres certainly don't live forever in the physical sense," she scoffed. "Your spirit and mind do. But kids see the vampyre movies or read those books, and they think maybe they'll meet someone out there who can initiate them and let them live forever and do superhuman things, too. It's so silly to make it look like vampyres have to have human blood all the time. I haven't had any for a while. Malcolm isn't into it, and there are other ways to handle it when I get the craving."

Specifically, Victoria said, she goes to the grocery store and buys a package of raw hamburger meat.

"I take the meat home and fry it just a little, so it's still really raw but also warm, and then I just suck the blood from it," she said, describing this as matter-of-factly as she might have discussed the weather. "It's very good. It's not the same as actual blood-drinking with someone else, but it gets me through the craving. And it's certainly safer, because of AIDS and everything. You have to be really careful about that if you're a vampyre."

If Malcolm doesn't change his mind about giving blood-drinking a try, Victoria said, she can settle for getting her blood from hamburger meat a while longer. She and Malcolm would like to leave Chicago and settle on the West Coast, but they don't have enough money yet. Victoria doesn't make much at her job, and twenty-four-year-old Malcolm's band has trouble getting booked into better-paying bar jobs because the other members are all fifteen or sixteen, too young to even get into the places where performers get more than a few dollars for a night's work.

"I wouldn't mind getting into the music business myself," Victoria added, "but in administration of some kind, not as a performer. Manager would be good, or something on the computer side."

Victoria communicates with other vampires and vampire wannabes by computer. She says America Online has helped her make many new friends.

"The important thing is to help them understand what vampyres really are," she said. "I want to dispel the old Hollywood notions. We're going to work one person at a time. I think it can happen. Society as a whole is becoming more open-minded. Things like body-piercing are the norm when having anything other than your ears pierced a few years ago was considered bizarre."

Meanwhile, Victoria said, she's proud to be a vampire.

"Just understand that blood-drinking is a thing I do, but it doesn't obsess my life," she concluded. "Help us get rid of the vampyre stereotype. Vampyres aren't murdering fiends. We're really very nice people, you know."

*"Once I'm sucking up their blood, they forget the pain right away. Trust me. They forget it. I'm kissing and suckling and licking this person. It's an erotic thing. They're enjoying themselves. It's hard not to."*

DARK ROSE

# 6
## *The Sexual Vampire*

The original vampires of mythology were mostly a sexless bunch. They were physically repulsive and took their blood by brute force, often from children or animals. Michelle Belanger of Shadowfox Publications says simply, "The folkloric vampire is a monster."

The vampires we met all across the country weren't monsters. Each had a healthy interest in sex, and for several, Dark Rose and Cayne in particular, sex was an intrinsic part of most blood-drinking activity. Christine Darque believed she was bitten by a vampire during sex. Victoria had her first blood-drinking experience while making love. Liriel said many of her blood-drinking correspondents considered sex and vampirism to be irrevocably linked. Gremlin, of course, insisted he conducted his psychic vampirism exclusively via sex.

Belanger said the Polidori/Stoker/Rice literary legacy was largely responsible for the shift in public perception of the vampire's potential for seductive qualities, and thus for the focus of real modern-day vampires on sex.

"*Dracula* in particular was written by Stoker in the Victorian era," she explained. "Stoker wrote a porn novel without ruffling a petticoat. He took the whole sex act, and instead of a penis you have a fang. Penetration occurs at the neck. You've got the whole orgasmic thing, and the bodily fluid exchanged is blood."

Martin Riccardo agreed—sort of.

"I have found there often are sexual connotations in the old legends," he argued. "Look at the gypsy lore about vampires— some people believe the gypsies may have brought the vampire legends into eastern Europe. They call the vampire the 'mulo,' which simply means 'the dead' in the gypsy language. It is often the dead husband or dead lover who comes back to visit the woman. The gypsies believed they came back out of a sexual appetite."

Still, Riccardo added, modern writers, filmmakers, and vampire voyeurs have added a lot of sexual allure to the vampire image.

"Now, where vampirism might have started as a terrifying superstition, over the centuries it's evolved into a dark romantic fantasy," he said. "So where most blood-drinkers, people identifying themselves as vampires, are concerned, my feeling is that this is kind of a sexual fetish, where blood-drinkers feel an amorous, emotional response to the blood. And that can be very positive, because in most cases the blood-drinkers have a steady, monogamous relationship where they practice this, often because of fear of AIDS. This is why I say that it is basically a nonharmful, nonthreatening practice, simply an extension of some people's sexuality, even though they won't always acknowledge it as part of their sexuality."

That frustrates Vlad, who believes too many blood-drinkers identifying themselves as vampires are just acting out their sexual blood fetishes.

"Look, if you drink blood and it's a sex deal, don't call yourself a vampire," he insisted. "You're a blood fetishist. Admit it, dig it, live it."

Yet Vlad, who drinks his wife's blood once a week, agreed all his own initial experiences with blood-drinking, which occurred during his teen years as a member of various rock-and-roll bands, happened during sex, too.

"Blood-drinking only took place during sex early on because it was the only opportunity," Vlad recalled. "You're in a city, here's a girl, she's hot, you go for it. But that was pre-AIDS."

Like Riccardo, Vlad believes the AIDS crisis has scared vampires of every persuasion into monogamy.

"AIDS changed everything," he said. "I was lucky, and I plan to stay that way. To be a blood-drinker now you have to be monogamous. Anyway, I don't believe it's a sexual act. It doesn't get me off."

El Paso's Cayne Presley said sex is almost always part of her vampirism, but as a preliminary.

"Basically, for the blood-drinking to be its best you have to totally relax the other person," she said. "With me, I use sex to break the ice. Once sex is initiated, people feel closer to you, and after sex they're very relaxed. I never drink blood from anyone who doesn't want me to, but even if they do want me to, the first few times they're nervous. The sex helps with that."

Her male lovers usually find postcoital blood-drinking to be an extension of the sex act, Cayne said.

"More often than not, the donors find sexual pleasure because of the sucking sensation," she explained, adding that she always takes blood from the large veins in the crooks of her lovers' arms. "For them it's almost, I'm told, like the sensation of a girl sucking a guy's private part. It arouses them terribly. Often they want sex again right afterward. And yes, we do it."

She doesn't have to drink blood every time after having sex, Cayne noted.

"The sex can be good on its own," she said. "But if I know I'm going to get what I want most after it, then the sex itself is heightened for me."

Dark Rose in Orlando said that she assumed every vampire and donor participated in blood-drinking acts for sexual gratification. Surveys she's conducted through her very R-rated *Dark Rose Journal* confirmed her suspicion.

"I set up a questionnaire, and it's all very sexual and erotic to everybody," Dark Rose said. "I can't imagine taking blood just to drink it. For what purpose? Some people say they do it because it gives them power. But that's just alien to me because it's never, as far as I'm concerned, been anything but sexual."

Like Vlad and Victoria, Dark Rose did her first adult blood-drinking during sex.

"It wasn't like we were sitting there over coffee, it was during a sexual moment," she remembered. "In the heat of passion, I decided to go for it and asked, 'Do you mind a little pain?' I used a razor blade. It wasn't right there. I had to get up and get it."

She keys her blood-drinking to whatever sexual pace is otherwise involved, Dark Rose continued.

"It depends on the sexual situation," she said. "I can do it until the blood stops coming. It could be a really long, romantic thing, it could be just a quick thing during intercourse, there's no specific time. I tell them beforehand that it's going to be a little painful. It'll hurt just for a second. And once I'm sucking up their blood, they forget the pain right away. Trust me. They forget it. I'm kissing and suckling and licking this person. It's an erotic thing. They're enjoying themselves. It's hard not to."

In her *Dark Rose Journal*, she constantly emphasizes practicing "safe" vampirism, which means being certain donors are disease-free before taking their blood.

"I am horrified to think there's anybody out there taking blood indiscriminately in light of the whole AIDS thing," she said, her voice rising in anger. "I try to push that as much as I can, to be responsible. My god, I had some people who were practicing blood-drinkers saying, 'Oh, didn't you hear? You can't get AIDS that way.' I just wanted to smack them. What were they spreading those lies for? Of course you can!"

But Cayne said she didn't let the possibility of contracting AIDS ever stand in her way if she felt like drinking blood.

"The way I look at it is, whatever happens to me later is just going to happen," she said. "I don't think I'll get AIDS, and most of the time I am careful, like I'll use guys who donate plasma regularly, because those donation places test them for everything. But sometimes I won't."

Those times, Cayne said, usually occur when she picks up a new donor at a bar.

"Maybe I've gone in just because I want to have a drink and be by myself, but guys do come over," she said, smiling widely at memories she didn't specifically describe. "If one's persistent, really persistent, I might say to him, 'Well, I have a certain interest, and if you'll give me what I want, I'll give you what you want.' They always think I mean drugs, and they'll say, 'Yes, yes, I can get you anything you want, just tell me what it is.' And I say, 'You've got what I want inside you. I'm a blood-drinker.' And they might go away, but sometimes they'll stay, and then I do give them what they want, and they do give me what I want."

Even though some of her bar pickups were turned on by the thought of having their blood drunk, Cayne noted more were repulsed.

"That's fine, because I don't want blood from anybody who's not completely willing," she insisted. "I know the few times I've talked someone into it, and they were sorry later, I regretted it, too."

Christine Darque of Indianapolis doesn't even drink blood. But after she began adopting a vampire persona, including sleeping in a coffin and having permanent fangs attached to her incisors, she found it tougher to connect with new men friends.

"Once you get into it, the vampire thing, then you should tell people up front what you're about," she said. "Right now, I've got these blind dates coming. I've just finished a relationship. Now everybody's trying to set me up with these guys. And they call, and I have to tell them right off I have fangs. I have to ease into this. I say, 'I sleep in a coffin and have fangs.' Once I get that over with, if they're still talking to me, okay. But I don't want to frighten some guy who's a blind date if he comes to my door, and the first thing he notices are my teeth, and then he sees my casket. He's gonna run out the door about ninety miles an hour. Everybody should be straight up and honest about what they do and what they're into, so you won't have these little misunderstandings going on in your life."

Of course, being honest can also destroy a relationship. Christine, who estimated she corresponds with about seventy-five vampires around the country, said that was the case for one of her penpals.

"An example would be my friend Ingrid," she said. "She's a blood-drinker and was into it, basically, but it wasn't the only thing she was into. In fact, we got all through that in our first couple of letters and started writing more about hideous high school experiences and fun stuff. Got way off the topic of vampires and stayed off it. But she met this man and dated him for a while, and the subject of vampires and blood-drinking came up. She'd decided she was going to tell him about it. But he started saying the whole vampire thing was so stupid and blah, blah, blah. She went ahead and told him she was a blood-drinker anyway, and he was extremely repulsed by this. He said, 'I can't believe I kissed lips that somebody's blood has been on!' And he just got up and walked out. Totally destroyed the relationship."

Many vampire wannabes who have approached real blood-drinkers want to be "initiated" into The Life because they think it involves nonstop sex, an idea they've gleaned from books and movies.

"At one time I would go out in a long cloak with the hood and the makeup and the fangs and be passing out demo tapes or whatever," Vlad recalled. "These two guys came up, and one actually said, 'Do you know Lestat?' The other guy goes, 'No, he looks like the kind of guy who would like Marius.' They were dead serious. They were talking about Anne Rice's characters. I said to them, 'They're pussies,' meaning Lestat and Marius, and walked away, because that was all I could think of to say. What I should have told them was, 'Being Lestat is not going to empower you. You're not going to get all the babes. You're not going to turn into mist and go through keyholes and look at women's naked bosoms.' It's not like a movie, damn it."

Still, Michelle Belanger suggested, it would be wrong to conclude vampirism isn't about sex, or at least sensuality.

"I'm not sure what their morality or ethical code is, but it seems to be a very sensual approach to life, almost, 'If it feels good, do it,'" she said. "Not necessarily sexual—most of them are not phallocentric. They're more into lying there with their hands on one another. A couple of groups we're familiar with in Cleveland are like that. They're touch-oriented. And, of course, there are psychic vampires I know who keep coitus and the vampiric act very separate."

As with non-blood-drinkers, vampires are straight, bisexual, or gay. Dark Rose is openly bisexual; Cayne has had lesbian sex but just as a trade-off to get blood. Vlad is vehemently heterosexual. Christine Darque numbers vampires of all sexual persuasions among her correspondents. "Of three men who write to me a lot, two are gay," she said. "With straight guys, I guess there sometimes are ones proposing to be a vampire to get laid. But women, hell. A woman should not have a problem getting laid no matter what she's into. You can do that anywhere. Now some women claiming to be vampires, I think they're more into the romantic idea of meeting Lestat. For those types, it's all fairy-tale stuff."

Part of the fairy tale, every real vampire insisted, was the fiction of the vampire always taking blood from the victim's throat. In fact, preferred drinking areas include the crook of the arm, the inner thigh, the back, the wrist, and, for Dark Rose, a spot about one inch above her donor's left nipple, whether she is drinking from a male or female. Incisions, usually one or two inches long and less than a quarter-inch deep, are made with razor blades, scalpels, or other sharp instruments. Tearing donor flesh with teeth is not something real vampires do.

"You usually pick spots that are erotic, very sexual, to you and still can be covered up by clothes afterward," Dark Rose said.

But for the vampire to drink from these spots, usually the donor has to remove some or all of his or her clothing, which wouldn't necessarily be the case if, as in movies, vampires drank blood exclusively from necks. Then, too, the vampires much prefer drinking the blood directly from the donors' bodies instead of draining off a small amount and drinking it from a cup or other container. And this, of course, means they have to put their mouths on the donors' flesh and suck.

"How can that not be sexually exciting?" Cayne wanted to know.

Psychologists sometimes speculate that excessive adult interest in sex can be the result of childhood sexual experiences. Dark

Rose and Cayne, the two most avid sexualists among the vampires, both said they had been sexually abused as children, Dark Rose once by her adoptive father and Cayne repeatedly by friends of her parents. Both were sexually active as teenagers before they formally accepted their vampiric personas. But both also noted their cravings for blood were present before they were molested.

"Needing blood is just part of my nature," Dark Rose said. "That doesn't have anything to do with what my father did to me."

Cayne believes, in part, that her particular brand of sexual vampirism might be related to the childhood rapes.

"When I'm having sex and taking the guy's blood, I'm absolutely the one in charge," she said. "I guess it could be a way of my taking control and doing something to someone instead of having something done to me. But I don't analyze it, really. I do it because I like it so much."

Liriel endlessly analyzes every aspect of vampirism, her own and that of others. She expects to soon launch another Vampirism Research Institute Survey, this one focusing on sex.

"That's because I've had a lot of people mention sex," she said. "I'm going to call the new survey 'Sex and the Vampire' since I'm really curious about finding out how much of the interest out there is based on sex."

Liriel was the only blood-drinker interviewed who said she believed most practicing vampires weren't first introduced to the act during sex.

"I don't think I've had one person tell me he or she was initiated that way," Liriel insisted. "They don't talk about having a strong sexual attraction to vampirism."

Yet the very successful *Dark Rose Journal* is almost completely devoted to tales of vampire sex—"Vampire erotica," Dark Rose said with a laugh. Though she encourages subscribers to send in their own fictional tales, Dark Rose and her fiancé, Avery, currently write most of the articles using their own names and pseudonyms.

Most of what they write is sexual. One of the *Journal's* regular features is "The Dark Rose Inn," a pretend spot where proprietor Dark Rose welcomes guests open to any and all voluptuous adventures.

In the Autumn 1995 *Journal,* Dark Rose graphically described an imagined encounter at the inn between her and a seventeen-year-old maid named Sonya.

"I savor the sweet taste of her blood as I let it linger on my lips before swallowing every last precious drop," she wrote. "Then I'll move my bloodstained lips up to her soft and supple mouth. As I force some of her own blood back down her throat, she'll begin to move her slender body the way that humans do when they become highly aroused. She will beg me for more bloody kisses. I will bite into my lip and let my vampiric blood slide down her throat. Of course, that will not be enough to sate her growing hunger. She will beg me for more of my powerful nectar. I, of course, will have to deny her more than a few drops of my blood. I will bring her to the point of orgasm many, many times. Her exhausted human shell will offer me anything in return for one more kiss. I will have dark pleasure after dark pleasure with my little human doll. I will take from her the glorious life-giving food of the immortal gods, over and over again. She will never know a dream or fantasy that will bring her this kind of ecstacy. My vampire kisses and caresses will forever remain the most erotically pure experience of her human life."

Michelle Belanger warned that desire to imitate some explicit vampire acts can go beyond accepted norms of sexuality. In her opinion, "vampirism, as the expression of the dark side of human desire, not only embodies the socially acceptable heterosexual act but also the less accepted and therefore more threatening sexual forces of rape, necrophilia, sado-masochism, and bestiality."

Dark Rose, too, is concerned that some readers might take her sexual fantasies-in-print too seriously. In each issue of the *Dark Rose Journal*, she always includes a section called "Fine Print" on the inside front cover. It reads in part:

"This Journal is dedicated to exploring the pleasures of the Dark. These do not include any manner of violent acts, kinkiness with unwilling parties, sexual misconduct, exploitation of the young or innocent, or illegal activities of any kind, even if the only aggrieved party might be a right-wing extremist, left-wing extremist, or politician...Those who do not enjoy the Journal and do not wish to participate in the lifestyle it describes should simply put it down and not read the damn thing."

That same philosophy is what Cayne believes should dictate the reactions of non-blood-drinkers to vampiric sex.

"Whatever we are, vampires or whatever they want to call us, we are what we are and we do what we do," Cayne concluded. "If it sounds good to you, you can probably find someone and try it. If it doesn't, have fun your way and we'll have fun our way. But don't tell us we're wrong, because what we do feels so *wonderful.*"

*"I take the blood when my donor is nice and relaxed. It hurts him maybe for a moment like a bee sting. I have to be careful not to suck too hard because the vein can collapse. It's hard to stop, but I can't take too much— maybe I take half a pint at a time. It's like drinking the finest wine you can imagine. Oooh—I'm getting thirsty just thinking about it."*

CAYNE PRESLEY

# 7
## Cayne

After about ninety minutes of discussing her vampiric lifestyle, thirty-seven-year-old Cayne Presley couldn't stand it anymore. She excused herself, jumped up from the king-size water bed where she'd been sitting cross-legged, and rushed to the kitchen of the modest tract house where she lived on the southern edge of El Paso.

Cayne threw open the refrigerator door and extracted a tightly capped bottle. The bottle had a white paper label taped on it, identifying it as "Cayne's Medicine."

"Sometimes I have to keep my boyfriend's grandson, who's six," she explained, her voice getting shaky with barely controlled need. "I have to put a label on the bottle so he won't open it by mistake."

The bottle contained a pint of cow's blood Cayne had bought the day before from a cooperative butcher. She drinks animal blood when the craving is on her and human blood isn't immediately available. Reverently, Cayne poured a large measure of the blood into a clear glass shaped like a somewhat smaller brandy snifter. She capped the bottle, returned it to the refrigerator, then cupped the glass in her hands and began to gently roll the blood around, warming it with her palms the way drinkers often warm vintage brandy.

"I have to get it warm this way. I found out the hard way blood can't be microwaved," she muttered, her concentration almost completely taken away from her visitor and focused on the blood in the glass.

Cayne scuttled back to her private room, where she had the water bed and her Anne Rice books and her various bits and pieces of vampire paraphernalia. She crouched on the water bed and continued rolling the blood in the glass between her palms. As it warmed, the sharp blood scent was almost suffocating. It permeated the entire room.

Finally, when she couldn't wait any longer, Cayne raised the glass to her lips with slightly trembling hands. She took a deep drink, sighing with relief. A drop of blood beaded at the corner of her mouth and seemed ready to drip down her chin. Deftly, she caught it with a lizard-quick swipe of her tongue. She closed her eyes and cooed wordlessly with pleasure.

"That's so much better," she said softly. "I just had to have some. Now we can talk some more. Where were we?"

※

Cayne Presley had returned to her birthplace of El Paso eighteen months earlier, driven to come back after years of relatively aimless wandering by a curiosity to see if her old hometown had changed much from the stodgy place she remembered.

"I sort of had a normal childhood," she said. "My father was mostly a truck driver, my mother stayed home. No brothers or sisters. Just me. From the time I was little, I wanted to be a movie star. And I always liked to wear black. I still always wear black. People who do that are supposed to be so depressive. They say if you wear black all the time you're a dark sort of personality. Well, I'm not that way now, and I wasn't then. I'm happy, I smile."

Cayne said her "sort of normal childhood" was marred around the age of nine, when she was sexually abused by adult friends of her parents. In a second interview, she said she was abused by an uncle.

"I never, ever thought about saying anything to my parents," she said. "I was always a child who was obedient, and it didn't occur to me that the ones doing this to me would get in more trouble than I did if I told."

About the same time, though, Cayne discovered something else about herself.

"Also when I was nine, I was with a guy who was a little older who accidentally cut his finger," she remembered. "That was my first taste of blood. He let me suck on the cut. It was so great. I just gently sucked on it. After that, I wanted blood all the time. I couldn't go up to people yet and ask them to donate, so what I'd do is sneak raw meat from my parents' refrigerator to suck on. They caught me a couple of times, but I was also watching vampire movies all the time, so they thought it was just a phase. It wasn't. I identified with vampires. We had so much in common. My skin is naturally pale and sensitive to sunlight. And, of course, there was the need for blood."

The blood cravings intensified as Cayne grew older. She quit high school around the tenth grade, leaving, she noted, because a teacher had made advances toward her and several other girls. School really didn't matter to her very much. She'd found her first regular blood donor and was swept up in the excitement of continuously fulfilling what she thought of as "the vampire nature" within herself.

"I am not bisexual," Cayne insisted. "This was the only time I had sex with another female. She had been my best friend in high school. We were seventeen. She wanted to have sex with me, which I wasn't interested in. But I wanted blood. She said she loved me enough to let me drink her blood. I thought if she would make that sacrifice for me, I should make a sacrifice for her. So we each did what we wanted, and it was a thrill for both of us, though in two different ways. I really didn't get anything out of the sex with her but frustration. I was having sex with guys, too, though. My girlfriend and I would go out riding horses together and do everything we did out in the open air."

Cayne went on to the Texas state capital, attending Austin Community College after she'd earned her G.E.D. in El Paso. She liked Austin, which seemed more liberal than El Paso, and she got up the nerve to find a butcher who'd sell her animal blood. Her opportunities to find other human blood donors lessened when she met and married another college student.

"I was just eighteen," she chuckled. "He was very straight-laced. I couldn't think of telling him about my drinking blood. I guess I got married because I wanted some emotional security. My girlfriend in El Paso and I had a falling-out about my marriage. She found another lover. But I didn't have another donor."

Cayne's marriage lasted ten years. Eventually, she said, her prim husband proved less conservative than she'd imagined.

"A friend of his got him drunk and talked him into wife-swapping," she said. "He found out he liked it, and we would go around to these clubs where you swap spouses for the night. There are a lot more of them than most people realize. So we did this, but I still couldn't tell him about needing to drink blood. I went to the butcher secretly for that. After a while, when my husband would go on business trips, I'd have lovers while he was gone. I did tell them about blood-drinking. They let me do it. It was so wonderful to have real human blood again! This is where I learned to take the blood from the crook of the arm. Before with my girlfriend we'd done the finger-cutting. Well, I eventually did tell my husband about the lovers, though not the blood-drinking, and he went bonkers! I couldn't understand why he thought he could fool around on the road—I mean, I'd call his room and girls would answer—and take me to swingers' clubs and then get upset because I was having lovers, too."

Cayne's husband ordered her to meet with a therapist "to cure me of whatever was wrong. I didn't tell the therapist about the blood-drinking, but I did tell him what my husband was like. The therapist told me I ought to get out of the marriage, so I did."

Cayne stayed in Austin, working at a midlevel job with a computer company and continuing to drink blood from her lovers. Eventually she got a job at the Department of Public Safety working as a DWI file clerk. The job was less important than off-duty blood-drinking. Having started doing it again, Cayne intended never to stop. She began refining her techniques for maximum vampiric benefit.

"I found it was best after sex," she said. "I take the blood when my donor is nice and relaxed. It only hurts him maybe for a moment like a bee sting. I have to be careful not to suck too hard because the vein can collapse. It's hard to stop, but I can't take too much—maybe I take half a pint at a time. It's like drinking the finest wine you can imagine. Oooh—I'm getting thirsty just thinking about it."

To open her donors' veins, Cayne would use triangular-shaped needles purchased from a veterinarian. After making the puncture, she'd close her lips over the wound and suck. After she'd branched out to finding other donors besides her regular lovers, she occasionally ran into someone who'd let her drink his blood but didn't want her to suck it with her mouth directly on his body.

"Then I'd attach a little tube to the needle and drink it up through that," she said, grinning at the thought.

Cayne felt comfortable thinking of herself as a vampire. Though she loved the genre movies and Anne Rice books, she didn't imagine herself as someone who might become immortal or have supernatural powers because of blood-drinking, though she still believes—and hopes—that somewhere some vampires might exist who possess these traits. Cayne simply had a compulsion to drink human blood, as much and as often as possible. If that defined a vampire, then she was one.

"Besides, people had told me all my life, 'Wow! Are you a vampire?'" Cayne said. "Well, okay, so maybe I was. What worried me was, could it be I was the only one in the world? I always felt there had to be more vampires. If there weren't, why would people read about them so much? I started researching, talking to people, trying to get an idea where they could be."

Cayne didn't find any other vampires, but she did discover that potential blood donors could often be encountered in Austin's public libraries.

"You can go up and talk to anyone about anything in libraries," she said. "It was still hard to find someone willing, so I started saying 'Give me what I want and I'll give you what you want.' I would say this to guys in libraries or in bars. I was really attracted to tall, thin guys with long, black hair. I still am. They really do it for me. But blood attracted me more. And if I had to have some, it was fine with me to let some guy have sex so I could drink his blood."

Cayne doesn't consider trading sex for blood the same as selling sex for money.

"I wouldn't do that," she insisted. "But the body is to be used. It's a tool like anything else. If your body can get you what you have to have, like blood, then use it. For blood, it's a fair trade."

Cayne said her happy life in Austin took a turn for the worse when her ex-husband started coming around. There were various problems. At one point her house was burned down. She moved on, ending up in Tallequah, Oklahoma, where she met and briefly married her second husband, a sixty-seven-year-old Native American.

"He was a full Cherokee, and I loved him more than life itself," Cayne said, her chirpy voice briefly turning mournful. "He died of a heart attack before we'd even been married a year. He understood my blood-drinking. He let me drink his blood. I was amazed he could be so open at his age. But he was. He was the love of my life."

After his death, Cayne embarked on a rough odyssey that took her all over the country. She hitchhiked around for more than six months, scraping up money at odd jobs and wandering without any real destination in mind. It was a bad time, made worse by the inability to satisfy her blood cravings.

"I had to go without that full-bodied flavor of blood, but I didn't have any donors or any money to go to a butcher shop if I even could find one," Cayne moaned. "As a result, I got very, very sick. One time I got so desperate I killed a bird to get its blood. Birds' blood is awful! I never did that again."

Like Liriel in Seattle, Cayne even tried cutting herself and drinking her own blood.

"But I barely bleed," she grumbled.

Cayne had to use what little money she had for normal food. Finally, the blood addiction overcame her when a driver who'd given her a ride tossed her a five-dollar bill after letting her out in a small town whose specific name and location she can't recall.

"I went to this butcher shop and bought a steak," she said. "It was nice and bloody. Getting it saved my life, I'm certain."

Eventually Cayne's ramblings took her to New Orleans, which she enjoyed. Anne Rice's territory fascinated her, but instead of settling down, she found herself curiously fixated on El Paso. Both her parents were dead, never aware their little girl's blood-drinking phase wasn't a phase. But Cayne wanted to revisit the city where her blood-drinking began.

"At the time the movie *The Crow* was released, and I loved it," she said. "So I got to El Paso and dressed up as The Crow to get the movie some publicity. I was walking to a movie theater, and Jose drove by and offered me a ride. We've been living together just about ever since. This is his house."

Cayne's new man was much more conservative than her second husband. Her blood-drinking made him nervous; he wouldn't let her drink his. When she started frequenting butcher shops to get animal blood instead, Jose didn't want her to drink that in front of him.

"So I have to do it when he's asleep or else when he's in the bathroom, and I know he's going to be in there a long time," she said. "He doesn't want me to tell his whole name or anything else about him."

So Cayne settled down in El Paso. She was hired at one of the city's Lee jeans factories and given the job of stitching on back pockets. Her work hours were 5:00 P.M. to 2:00 A.M., which suited her exactly.

"If I can avoid the sun, great," Cayne enthused. "The nighttime is my time. I sleep from 7:00 A.M. to noon or 1:00 P.M. The work schedule is fine."

Soon Cayne made the acquaintance of another butcher. As she became a regular customer, he began saving specific kinds of blood for her, depending on availability and her own appetite on different days.

"Pork blood is very smooth," Cayne said, speaking with the confidence of a longtime connoisseur. "My favorite is human. Humans vary in the taste of their blood, depending on what they've eaten. If they've had garlic, I can tell. Beef blood also has a very distinct flavor. And as for deer blood! A lot of people say humans can't stomach deer blood. But I have a hunter friend, and I go out with him and take the blood from the deer he kills. It tastes tart, gamy, wild. When I get enough, I even feel a little heady."

As much as she savored the blood of various animals, though, Cayne still had her deepest craving for blood sucked directly from the warm, living bodies of human donors. With Jose refusing to participate, she had to look elsewhere in El Paso. Elsewhere turned out to be at another Lee manufacturing plant.

"There was a security guard at this plant, and we spent some time getting, I thought, really, really close," she said. "I hated remembering what it had been like going without blood from a regular donor for so long, like when I had to kill the bird. I didn't want that to happen again, so I started developing a relationship with the guard, trying to form an emotional attachment, so that if the time came when I had to move out from my boyfriend's, I could go on to be lovers with this other guy and regularly have the human blood again. I told him about my blood-drinking. It got him all excited."

At the same time, Cayne continued what had previously been a fruitless search for other vampires or people who knew where she could contact other vampires. Someone in an El Paso bookstore—again, her memory for details is hazy—gave her some addresses. Eventually she got in contact with Christine Darque in Indianapolis. Cayne loved Christine's letters and videos, and was especially taken with her new friend's tale of being bitten by a vampire named Christopher.

"Oh, I would love to meet Christopher and be with him," Cayne sighed. "Christine sent me a videotape she'd had secretly taken of him. He's got long, dark hair, and he is so, so wonderful. Of course, Christine herself is not a vampire. She has the fangs and sleeps in a coffin, but she doesn't drink blood.

We've become good friends through the mail. I love her so much I'd have sex with her if she really wanted, but I hope she wouldn't. I'll bet we could really party together. I still very much want to talk with other vampires, but it makes me feel good that I know Christine is out there, and because of knowing her, I know about Christopher, too."

Back in El Paso, though, Cayne's attention had to turn to the Lee plant security guard.

"Until Jose and I were over, I wanted to keep the other guy and me just friends," she said. "But this security guy became too possessive. He wanted to run away with me and for us to get married. I told him I wasn't ever again going to be anyone's wife. But I did share blood with him not too long ago. I drank his, and I let him drink some of mine. It was the first time I'd done that. It was great! But I didn't let everything become completely sexual, though he wanted to. And it could have become very sexual, but I couldn't allow it because of Jose."

Cayne's fidelity cost her. Angrily, the guard went to the Lee plant where she worked and told everyone that Cayne Presley was a blood-drinking vampire.

"I got to work that night, and everybody was looking at me funny," Cayne said. "At the meal break this girl who was my good friend came over. I asked her what was the matter. She said, 'We've all heard the rumor you drank something unusual.' I thought, 'Oh, shit!' and I asked her, 'Blood, right?' She said, 'Do you drink blood?' and somehow I found myself saying, 'On occasion.'"

Around the country, vampires call the moment they publicly identify themselves as blood-drinkers "coming out of the coffin." Cayne found her coming-out to be a great relief, especially in light of her friend's reaction.

"She smiled and said, 'Wow!' and was just totally tripped out by it," Cayne said. "She's been married for ten years, but she told me she's really interested in blood-drinking, and she's come over while my boyfriend was out of town. We're going to share blood, I think. It would be a wonderful thing. We probably won't have sex. I don't think she wants to because she is married. But if she really wanted, I guess I would."

The rest of her co-workers at Lee, Cayne said, have pretty much accepted her for what they've discovered she is.

"It's so great to have it out in the open," she enthused. "No one has come up and threatened me or anything. And it's impossible for them to think I'm a bad, evil person because I'm naturally so cheerful and nice. I'd do anything to help anybody. Even my boss has been fine. He feels about it the same way he feels about someone's sexual inclinations—'Whatever you are and whatever you do, leave it at home.'"

So Cayne has recently fed on human blood again, will probably have it regularly from now on, her co-workers know about her vampirism, and she's living with her boyfriend Jose.

It's not enough.

"I would very much like to meet other blood-drinkers, talk to them, get to know them," Cayne said. "That's why I'm cooperating with this book. Maybe some others will read it and want to get in touch with me. You can print my address. Jose doesn't mind if I let you print the address, as long as when the letters come they have my name on them and not his."

Through Christine, Cayne has just begun to understand how vast the underground vampire network is, and how many other self-proclaimed vampires are also trying to meet fellow blood-drinkers. She's especially enthused about Vampires of America's *Vampire Theatre* videozine. She has a television and VCR at the foot of her water bed and often uses them to watch vampire movies or the videos Christine sends. *Vampire Theatre* would be great entertainment, she thinks.

More than any other vampire we interviewed, Cayne wanted to know everything all the other blood-drinkers had said. How old were they when they first tasted human blood? How often did they drink it now? And, most specifically, when they took blood from donors, where did they make their cuts on the donors' bodies, and how much blood did they drink?

"I know I've been doing this for quite a while, but I only know my own way," she admitted a bit sheepishly. "Someone else may know better methods. I think if I do meet another vampire, the first thing I'll want to talk to him or her about will be technique. Technique is so important."

And, possibly, Cayne thinks she might meet a vampire life partner.

"We could share sexual and blood relations the whole rest of our lives," she said. "To me, that would be the most incredible bond. How could you get any more intimate with someone? What would be really cool would be to have someone drinking from me at the very moment I'm drinking from him. My yearning for that is so strong I've had dreams about it. To drink the blood of someone you love while he drinks yours, well—"

That's when Cayne had to excuse herself to get a drink of blood.

After Cayne finished her drink, and after she'd carefully licked every remaining bit of blood from her lips and teeth, she pronounced herself ready to talk some more. Somehow drinking the blood had brightened her appearance. At thirty-seven, Cayne's about medium height and build with thick facial features and prominent teeth, though her incisors aren't especially long. Her skin, after a lifetime of dodging the sun, is quite pale. She's had some tough times, and the lines caused by them are apparent on her face and hands. Most of the blood-drinkers we met looked younger than their real ages, but Cayne did look thirty-seven. She's not at all unattractive, but except for her head-to-toe black clothing, Cayne isn't someone you'd glance at twice if you passed her in the aisle of a grocery store.

Refreshing herself with blood during our interview put an extra sparkle in Cayne's eye. Earlier while she talked, she'd slouched almost motionless on the water bed, swathed in a black cloak because she'd complained of feeling cold. Postblood, she shrugged the cloak off her shoulders and bounced up and down on her haunches while she chatted. Her cheeks were visibly flushed.

"I loved being able to answer the questions of my girlfriend at work," Cayne said. "She asked me things like, 'Doesn't drinking blood get your stomach upset?' Her husband doesn't know anything about us. And she's saying all the time now, 'I think I might like to try it.' She's going to love it. I think anyone would if they'd try it. A couple other people at work have sort of hinted they're interested, too. Maybe that guard's telling about me is going to be a really, really good thing. I think it will."

Even if things work out well in El Paso, though, Cayne doesn't think she's long for West Texas.

"I love New Orleans, and I plan to move back there just as soon as I can," she said. "I can't go yet because Jose and I are trying to get a little business started. But after we do, where he and I are concerned, all things must come to an end unless he does decide to come to New Orleans with me. And if he doesn't, well . . ."

Cayne doesn't know how she'll earn a living in New Orleans.

"I'll just do whatever it takes, like I always do," she said. "What I do for a living isn't that important, anyway. What matters is doing what's natural to me, following my nature. In New Orleans, or anywhere, I'll never stop drinking human blood. I can't give it up. I won't. Ever.

"You might as well ask me to give up breathing."

*"Now, I don't have any friends in this neighborhood. I'm obviously not Suzy Homemaker. At all. I don't cook, I don't do crafts with my kids, it's not in my nature. I'm not in the PTA thing. I try to be friendly, I try to talk to the neighbors and other parents, but what are we going to talk about? Once we get past all the surface stuff, then what?"*

DARK ROSE, WHO LIVES IN AN ATTRACTIVE,
MIDDLE-CLASS ORLANDO SUBURB

# 8
# The Social Vampire

The basic problem is simple. Most people think vampires are at best insane and at worst demon-spawned monsters, frantic to drain the blood from anyone unfortunate enough to catch their attention. Even so-called vampire "fans" are usually drawn by sexy movie and book stereotypes, imagining godlike beings who can bestow superpowers at the insertion of a fang and remaining completely oblivious to the problems faced by real human beings who happen to think drinking blood is as natural, and as necessary, as breathing.

Discovering their vampiristic tendencies early in life only seemed to make things worse, at least for the blood-drinkers we met.

Twenty-seven-year-old Dark Rose said she discovered her compulsion to drink human blood when she was five.

"But it wasn't something really out in the open," she said sadly. "The only blood I got was my own when I'd accidentally cut myself. It wasn't like I had a lot of access to people to ask them for blood when I was five. My mother says that for some reason when I was five my whole personality began to change, that I became a totally different person. Of course I did. After that, I had no friends. I never had any friends."

A sense of crushing social isolation afflicted many of the real-life vampires well into their adult lives.

"I've been the only vampire I've known of for so long," Cayne Presley said. "You can't imagine what a thrill it would be for me to talk to another one, just to know that, for once, I was talking to someone who might understand."

That same sense of being alone is what makes many blood-drinkers contact Martin Riccardo. Dozens of letters come to him every month begging for some sort of response that acknowledges somebody else somewhere has a similar blood-drinking obsession.

"I get letters from rural areas in places like Kansas, Iowa, Nebraska, whatever, and they all say, 'I have this craving for blood, and I feel very isolated and alone,'" Riccardo said. "But I get that same sense of isolation from people in population centers like New York. You see, actual blood-drinkers, as opposed to the casual 'vampire fans' who are just pretending to be vampires during a brief phase, find it very difficult to be accepted. There's a tremendous social taboo about drinking blood. People will not look past the fact that, beyond the blood-drinking, most so-called vampires tend to be average, normal people, often very friendly, very likable."

The first sense of isolation for real-life vampires invariably begins within their own families. Many of the vampires we visited have never told their parents or siblings about their blood-drinking. Those who are allowing their photographs to appear in this book think it will be okay because their relatives would never pick up a book about vampires.

Those who have tried to be open about themselves have generally received the same reaction as Gremlin.

"My mother was like, 'What, are you going to go around hurting people?'" he said. "And my wife basically put it to me that I didn't know how to deal with the real world, so I was going to hop into this fantasy zone and try to live that way."

Where childhood backgrounds of blood-drinkers are concerned, our short-term research matched Martin Riccardo's long-term findings: There's no single pattern besides loneliness to be discerned. Dark Rose and Cayne said they were sexually abused as children. Liriel, Gremlin, Dark Rose, and Vlad were raised in single-parent homes, but Victoria and Cayne weren't. Christine Darque, a non-blood-drinker who considers herself a "vampire victim," was also raised in a stable family environment.

"You can't come up with one type of childhood and say, 'There, that one causes children to grow up thinking they're vampires,' Riccardo said. "If you go to any group of people, you're going to find a certain number who were abused as children, a certain number who had a hard time growing up. But I've come across plenty who had perfectly normal, healthy childhoods."

Education is another matter. Among the vampires we met, only Victoria completed high school (the other exception was Christine Darque, the nonvampire).

"Well, how are you gonna stay in school if you don't have any friends, if you don't feel like you're like anybody else?" Liriel wanted to know.

Dark Rose and Gremlin recalled their parents being told by school officials that it might be better for the youngsters to complete their educations somewhere other than public school classrooms. Liriel's mother pulled her out of school because the other kids kept taunting her. Vlad quit school to join traveling rock bands.

At the same time, all the blood-drinkers seemed quite intelligent. Each was an avid reader, and several had hopes of publishing their own novels some day. Their problems coping with school stemmed from an inability to make friends, not *A's.*

"It comes back to fitting in, which is so important to adolescents," Riccardo said.

Unlike many socially excluded teenagers, though, most of the blood-drinkers we talked to didn't turn to drugs. Vlad admitted sampling the excesses of the road during his early touring days, and non-blood-drinker Christine Darque said she still gets drunk more often than she should. But Dark Rose spoke for the majority when she said, "Even though living totally in a world by yourself as a teenager is a pretty scary thing, I never did drugs, I never drank, and I could have done all that."

Most of the blood-drinkers were equally unable to function in church as well as school. That didn't mean they weren't religious in their own ways.

"It was very, very hard growing up in a strict Baptist home," Dark Rose recalled. "My mother made me go until I was eleven. The last time I went to church I was in Sunday school, and the class was talking about something. When it was my turn to talk I said, 'Well, I'm a witch.' The Sunday school teacher went, 'Huh?' Her mouth dropped open. I repeated, 'I'm a witch, and I don't buy into Christianity, so other than that I have no comment.' Of course, it got back to my mom rather quickly. I told her I didn't want to go because it made me ill to be there. I didn't connect with the people, they just seemed so weird to me. I didn't know how to really explain it. I do believe totally in a supreme spirit. I totally believe in the spiritual afterworld. I just don't give it a name."

Several other vampires said they believed in some higher power, but only Cayne identified that power as God. Of course, her approach to God was the polar opposite of the Christian Church.

"I pray, I talk to God, but I don't talk to Jesus," Cayne explained. "I mean, think about it. God is the supreme being, so that makes

Jesus the middleman. Why go through the middleman if you need something? Doesn't it make more sense to go to the top?"

Victoria and Dark Rose turned to Wicca. Each still believes in casting spells. None of the vampires now regularly attends a Christian church.

Yet all the blood-drinkers were quick to note they never would challenge the right of others to be Christians.

"Look, whatever you believe, fine," Vlad said. "If you consider yourself a Christian, if that is what makes sense to you, I believe you should be a Christian. I think anything you believe, if it gets you through the day and makes you a happy person and makes you treat the person next to you a little nicer than you otherwise would have, hey, I'll stand behind it. I'll never say Jesus Christ didn't walk the earth. If you believe he did, I will never tell you you're wrong."

Most vampires, Riccardo said, are accepting of anyone else's right to hold differing opinions about religion or society or virtually any other subject.

"These people know what it is to have a belief and to be mocked for it," Riccardo noted. "Almost without exception, I have found blood-drinkers to be extremely tolerant. They are broad-minded."

That was clearly the case concerning sexuality. Most of the vampires told us they know gay or lesbian blood-drinkers. Dark Rose herself is avowedly bisexual, though she's currently engaged to a man named Avery. Cayne had sex with one woman and said she would again if she, in turn, was allowed to drink her female partner's blood. None of the vampires in any way disparaged the sexual choices of anyone else.

Race was another matter. Every vampire we met, and each we were referred to, was white. Christine Darque said one of her seventy-five blood-drinking correspondents was Hispanic. Nobody ever said, "Yes, I know a black (or Hispanic, or Asian) vampire personally."

Christine Darque, Martin Riccardo, and Michelle Belanger, the three non-blood-drinkers who have spent years studying the vampire community, vehemently denied the lack of minority vampires is caused by any form of racism.

"I would say a higher proportion of vampires are white than is represented in the overall population," Riccardo said. "I have come across African-American, Hispanic, and Asian individuals who are into blood-drinking, but that's a very tiny percentage. In no way does this reflect racism, though. White vampires aren't trying to keep minority vampires out. I would suspect the minority percentage is so small because the cultural image of the vampire happens to be white. We have the occasional *Blacula* movie, or Eddie Murphy playing a vampire, but it's very hard to be a pale African-American, and vampires are supposed to be pale. So the part of the population that would respond and relate most to the vampire image would be Caucasian."

Belanger said in her personal experience, vampires are "mostly a white phenomenon. Blacks aren't drawn to vampirism. If they have any interest in blood, it's in blood magic, not drinking. And a lot of blacks are raised Christian. They never doubt it, they stay staunch believers."

None of the vampires claimed he or she would live forever. Several claimed, though, that blood-drinking would expand their life spans and keep them healthier and younger-looking. With the exception of Cayne, who looked her age but no older, all the blood-drinkers *did* look considerably younger than they really were. (In Dark Rose's case, this was a dramatic reversal from childhood, which will be explained in her individual chapter.)

Riccardo said many potential blood-drinkers are attracted to vampirism by its central theme of returning from the grave or, at least, the way vampires seem somehow beyond death.

"Death pervades the whole vampire image," Riccardo said. "He is the embodiment of death. He sleeps in a coffin. He's pale. He wears black clothing. There are all kinds of subconscious factors that make people want to learn some aspect of death and what might be possible after it. This does not mean people attracted to death imagery are suicidal. They're not. The vast majority of people who've written to me over the years are revitalized because of their experiences with or interest in vampirism. It's excited them, it's given them a new energy in life."

Michelle Belanger said the vampires she has met who claim an endless existence don't mean they've only had one very long life.

"The immortality as many of them interpret it is really serial immortality," she said. "They think of themselves as old souls. They've been reincarnated. They believe everybody is immortal because they're reincarnated. What separates the vampires from anybody else is, the vampire retains the memory of past lives, which accounts for the continuity that is their real definition of immortality."

The real vampires consider one-life-only immortality—at least in a single body—to be a lot less attractive than non-blood-drinkers might imagine.

"A lot of people who find out I'm a vampire want me to tell them that I'm really immortal," Dark Rose said. "Well, my spirit is, sure, everybody's spirit is. My body's not. And so many people who asked me the question about living forever don't want to hear that. But think about it—existing forever in the same body. How boring!"

Still, age is crucial. Liriel's research in particular indicated most people considering themselves vampires eventually grow out of that belief.

"Most of the people I've surveyed who said they were vampires ranged in age from fourteen to twenty-nine," she reported.

"The oldest was fifty-four. I think the next oldest was forty-four. I think for many it's like they get this total obsession with being a vampire for a while, and then they totally forget about it."

Dark Rose said aging is a natural way of winnowing out real vampires from wannabes.

"If (vampirism) isn't their true nature, then I agree, they'll grow out of it," she said. "The phrase I hear that tells me some-one really is sincere is, 'I've been this way since I was a child, tak-ing blood and taking lifeforce is a natural element to who I am.' If it's natural to them, that's what they'll always do. As they get older they're more comfortable with it, not tired of it."

Riccardo agreed that, in his experience, "most of the people are in their teens and twenties, but I've had people in many dif-ferent age groups. When it comes to fascination with vampires, that encompasses all ages."

One area of blood-drinker similarity, Riccardo said, is sensi-tivity to sunlight.

"Some of them have actually been diagnosed by their doctors as having a sun allergy," he noted. "I think it's very impressive they so much identify with the vampire image that they actually feel discomfort. Many of them wear sunglasses, even at night. Some have told me they have better night vision than most people—they claim almost like a cat. Many mention they love to wear black, just as a natural tendency. Don't you think it's interesting that these things are constantly repeated by blood-drinkers? I should also add that many, many blood-drinkers feel they have special psychic powers. They feel they can predict things, they can feel vibrations from people, read minds, have prophetic dreams."

Real vampires also feel uncomfortable with imposters.

"I hate the kids in capes," Gremlin said emphatically.

Dark Rose added she knows that, among her hundreds of jour-nal subscribers and America Online friends, "The vast majority are not like me. I don't think they practice blood-drinking or anything else. It can get old really fast. I realize most of these people are stuck in an Anne Rice fantasy. I adore Anne Rice, but Dark Rose is not a character. She's me, she's who I really am."

In the social pecking order, donors also occupy a lower rung. Even Liriel, whose blood-drinking was limited to her own body, was appalled when asked if she'd ever be a donor for someone else.

"No!" she blurted. "I wouldn't want to become another person's—oh, no. Never."

Victoria and Cayne had both let someone else drink their blood. But each emphasized that they allowed very little to be taken. Vlad said his wife had sampled a little of his blood on their wedding night, though not since. He regularly drinks her blood. Only Cayne yearned for a relationship with a blood-drinker where each would drink equally from the other.

"As a general rule, blood-drinkers and donors are exclusive roles," Riccardo said. "I have known a number of blood-drinkers who say they get a thrill of excitement from having blood taken from them, too, so in some cases it can go both ways. There are certainly many blood-drinkers who started by giving blood. Overall, blood-drinkers prefer to be the ones receiving rather than giving."

The role of taker simply fits the vampire personality better, Dark Rose observed.

"Nobody's ever asked me for my blood," she said. "It's always me taking theirs. If they'd asked, I probably would have said no. I think letting them drink my blood would have compromised my position. I have the attitude of, 'I'm the Dark Angel here, I'm the predator, not you.' So no, I don't want to. I'm not saying that's never going to happen. But as of right now, there's nobody I'd want to do that with."

Finding donors is a problem for some vampires and not others. When we talked to Dark Rose she was between regular donors, but she wasn't worried. Between her *Journal* subscribers and acquaintances over America Online, she said, "I have many offers on the table." Vlad had his wife, Cayne expected to be sharing blood soon with her girlfriend from work—until then, she was subsisting on animal blood—and Victoria was quite happy to be with non-blood-drinking Malcolm and suck an occasional near-raw chunk of hamburger meat.

But Riccardo said there are many vampires who are desperately seeking donors.

"Finding a donor can be done," he explained. "With all the vampire interest publications out there, there are potential donors who put out classified ads looking for vampires. But these people are often so far apart geographically that it can be hard for them to get together. That's another reason many blood-drinkers form long-term monogamous relationships. When you find someone willing to be your steady donor, you don't want to risk losing him or her and having to find someone else all over again."

Each vampire defined "regular" blood-drinking differently. Vlad was on the strictest schedule: He drank some of his wife's blood once a week, usually on Thursdays. When Cayne had a steady donor she drank as often as she could.

In an essay she titled "Angels of Darkness," Dark Rose wrote that "I must feed. If I don't draw energy from a human at least three or four times a week, I become very lethargic. It becomes hard for me to concentrate and function on a day-to-day basis...I have been drinking blood for so long now that I am physically addicted to it."

In our interview, Dark Rose said that whenever she's between regular blood donors, she feeds on psychic energy, which she can often draw out of other people without them knowing it. Gremlin said much the same thing. Cayne said if she went without blood too long, she actually became ill.

Everyone emphasized blood was only drunk from willing donors, and condemned any vampires who took blood by force.

"Those people aren't vampires, they're sick," Cayne said emphatically.

Riccardo said the media, eagerly buying into vampire stereotyping, often looks for ways to unfairly link blood-drinking violence with vampires.

"Newspaper articles or books sell more copies when they focus on a murder, a robbery, criminal activities in which there was some blood drunk," he said. "I can't say it any more simply than that the vast, vast majority of blood-drinkers have no interest in using force. They will always get voluntary donors. They are not psychotics or criminals. They crave blood. This is an orientation, a fixation, a lifestyle."

And it's a lifestyle that, as adults, they're eager to share in a way they couldn't as children. The underground communication system among vampires is extensive. Whenever we mentioned vampires we had met to blood-drinkers in other parts of the country, they usually knew of each other if they weren't personally acquainted or at least corresponding by letter or video. It's easy to assume that such a close-knit community can't be large, but this is a fallacy. Christine's regular correspondence with seventy-five different blood-drinkers, "vampire victims," and individuals who suspected they might be vampires was not considered an especially large number of penpals by Martin Riccardo or Michelle Belanger. Surveys done by Riccardo, Belanger, and Liriel McMahon routinely involved dozens of vampire respondents—and not always the same ones, either.

There are regular vampire conventions in cities like Seattle, New Orleans, Chicago, and Cleveland. Vlad, Riccardo, the Belangers, and Anne Rice's Fan Club have been some of the sponsors. There's talk in Chicago of starting up a vampire and vampire fan-related radio station, which would play the "Goth" music—heavy on The Cure and The Dark Theater—favored by the blood-drinkers.

Another interesting commonality among the vampires we interviewed was that every one of them we asked detested country music. "Disliked" is not a term that could be substituted. "Despised" might be. They assured us that all the other blood-drinkers they knew felt exactly the same way. Gremlin favored the louder rock bands: Soundgarden, Alice in Chains, Metallica. Dark Rose was the most eclectic in her musical tastes, with her special favorites including the Chieftains, Enya, the Beatles, Boston, Aerosmith, and several classical composers.

"I like all kinds, but I hate country," she declared.

All the assorted blood-drinkers watched vampire movies. A few of the older ones said they were also childhood fans of TV's *Dark Shadows* series. While they enjoyed *Interview With the Vampire* and others of its ilk, they also despaired of nonvampires who believed film fantasy somehow might translate into real-life fact. For several, Victoria in particular, it has become a lifelong project to tear down media stereotypes of vampires.

"Obviously no real blood-drinkers or vampires get involved in those films," she said. "Ripping people open, gulping all that blood—it just doesn't happen. The movies can be fun to watch, I agree. I've got *Bram Stoker's Dracula* on cassette right here. But people expect us to be like that."

Vlad, who's gone out of his way to publicly adopt the vampire persona as a marketing tool for his music, nevertheless has exhausted his patience for people who've bought into the movie vampire myth and want him to "turn" them.

"I've actually been offered brand-new cars to turn people into vampires," Vlad griped. "Well, if they're talking about these inhuman creatures, there's no such thing as vampires, please get it through your head. I'm sick of explaining this to them. There are no vampires like that; there're never gonna be any vampires like that; there are no goddamned vampires like that! It's a great story, a great myth. But a myth."

Sometimes from disgust with vampire stereotyping, sometimes from desire for a more socially acceptable indentity, many blood-drinkers don't want to be called vampires at all, even by people who know they're not the evil, superpowered creatures of film and fiction. Dark Rose prefers "Dark Angel." Gremlin wants to called a "Dark Soul." Victoria insists on "vampyre." Vlad, ever the showman in public and the pragmatist in private, says he likes the simple, descriptive name "blood-drinker."

Cayne likes being called a vampire.

Often, Christine said, pseudo-blood-drinkers who write to her claim to be vampires only as a starting point for expressing stranger fixations.

"I get some who start out okay, but then in their next letters go off talking about werewolves, ghosts, and demons," she said. "I had one girl tell me she was being raped by demons every night. I couldn't help but think it was someone in her family, actually."

Christine said she's careful to keep most of her correspondents at a physical distance.

"I use my real home address and not a post office box because I don't want to go to the post office every day," she explained. "That's been for, like, five years, and I've never had anyone just show up at my door. Now, I've had to talk a few people into not coming over. There was one girl who was real weird. She drank blood all the time, and she wanted to come over and drink blood with me. I wrote, 'Look. I don't think you should come over. We'll just keep writing. We can be real good friends through the mail, but we're stopping the buck right there.'

Out of her seventy-five pen-friends, Christine estimated, "Maybe five are serious, or maybe ten won't ever grow out of (blood-drinking). The others are pretty much kids in capes. I have one guy I write to who's forty-five. There are some housewives. In some ways I think maybe all of them are unbalanced. But they're lonely, and they're feeling things, and they need somebody who's going to understand what the heck they're talking about."

Christine was especially touched by one letter-writer.

"There was a woman who wrote me and said she had this terminal disease," Christine recalled. "She wanted to know more about vampires, maybe even get to be one, because she thought they might have immortal life and perfect health. She had a child, and she wanted to live and see the child grow up. So she wrote me hoping I'd be able to tell her that could happen. She was definitely sincere about it."

Many of the blood-drinkers said they could communicate better through the mail than in person. Often when out in public, especially in work situations, they felt the same sense of isolation they'd felt as kids in school.

None of Victoria's supervisors or co-workers in the Chicago mall where she's employed knows she's a vampire. Cayne was forced to "come out of the coffin" at the Lee jeans factory in El Paso and was gratified, at least up to the time when we interviewed her, with her co-workers' responses. Liriel said her friends and bosses at the King County offices considered her vampirism research "an interesting hobby." Gremlin works handling mail for a psychic line, a job that pretty much keeps him away from personal contact with customers. His goal, however, is to open his own tattoo parlor. Vlad uses vampirism as a marketing tool for his music. Besides working on her journal, Dark Rose doesn't have a job. Avery, her fiancé, brings home the paychecks.

Christine isn't a vampire, but she still has fangs permanently bonded to her teeth. She said that can make it hard to be successful in job interviews.

"When I hit a certain point I wanted to overhaul my entire life except for the vampire thing," she said. "I was working as a topless dancer in a bar, and I was to the point where I was drinking all the time. I was getting paid to sit there and drink and talk to men. So I wanted a change, and I had to go to job interviews, and then when I had them I had to try and talk without showing my fangs. The first job I got, the fangs gave everybody working there an off reaction, so I had to quit."

Christine got another job with a mail-order company whose members initially get a certain number of CDs for very little money and then have to buy several more at specified prices.

Her co-workers have spotted the fangs, she said, but she hasn't talked to anyone about them or her obsession with vampirism. Her job is to answer complaint letters from members. It's something she can do without being around anyone else.

If the vampires sometimes have trouble dealing with co-workers, they almost always have similar problems with neighbors. Some, like Cayne, just try to stay inside their own houses as much as possible. Living in a spiffy Orlando suburb, Dark Rose doesn't have that option. She has two children who attend a nearby elementary school, so she has to have a certain amount of interaction with other parents in the neighborhood whose kids play with hers. She doesn't wear fangs like Christine or Vlad, but with her strikingly lovely, pale features and jet-black hair, she doesn't look ordinary, either. Ultimately, despite her best efforts to at least partially fit in, Dark Rose has given up.

"Now, I don't have friends in this neighborhood," she said. "I'm obviously not Suzy Homemaker. At all. I don't cook. I don't do crafts with my kids. It's not in my nature. I'm not in the PTA thing. I try to be friendly, I try to talk to the neighbors and other parents, but what are we going to talk about? Once we get past all the surface stuff, then what?"

With the exception of Vlad, most of the blood-drinkers as kids had problems with their parents. Several have managed to make their peace with them as adults. Victoria had a good relationship with both her mother and father. Cayne's parents are both dead, but she said neither ever knew she had become a full-blown practicing vampire. Liriel is now so close to her mother and older sister that they may move to California together. When they do, she hopes to somehow regain communication with her father, whom she hasn't seen or even talked to in years.

"Maybe he'll read this book and find out where I am," Liriel said wistfully. "I know he remarried, actually, and had a son. I've never met my half-brother. I just know my father's in L.A. I'd like to do some catching up."

Gremlin said he sees his mother in Seattle every week, though she's not entirely pleased with his new affiliation with the Khlysty. After years of little communication, Dark Rose is back in touch with her mother. She hasn't told her mother about *The Dark Rose Journal* or her vampirism. She doesn't ever see her father, who she says once sexually molested her, or her older brother.

Non-blood-drinker Christine has given her very conservative parents some recent shocks, including seeing their daughter getting permanent fangs and discovering she sleeps in a coffin. Actually, Christine noted, so far only her father knows about the coffin-sleeping.

"My dad came to see me, and he comes in my room and sees this coffin," she said. "He goes, 'Where's your bed?' I go, 'There.' He says, 'Oh, has your mom seen that yet?' I said, 'Not yet.' She's not going to like it, I know. When she does, I bet she'll use the f-word for like only the third time in her whole life."

If nothing else, Christine's father handled the coffin news like a good sport. Skilled in all sorts of craftsmanship, he made his daughter a jewelry box shaped like a small coffin. She keeps it beside her coffin/bed, and smiles proudly when she shows it off to visitors.

Often estranged from at least some family members, limited professionally by appearance or personality or nocturnal lifestyle, condemned by outsiders buying into widely accepted stereotypes, modern-day blood-drinkers have no choice but to turn to each other for friendship. Letters have been the standard form of communication, but now computers and modems are rapidly replacing old-fashioned mail.

Dozens of vampire organizations around the country advertise in underground publications. Liriel McMahon's Summer 1995 *VRI News,* for instance, included an ad for "The National Gothic Singles Network." This included an 800-number to be called by "straight and gay" vampires, vampire fans, and musicians looking for work in bands. The same issue also included the address of "The Transylvanian Society of Dracula," which described itself as "an international educational-cultural organization of people interested in the myths and legends of Count Dracula...Join us in planning Dracula '97, the centennial celebration of the publication of Bram Stoker's novel."

While some of the groups were founded by vampires in search of fellow blood-drinkers, others certainly were the brainchildren of nonvampires who just wanted to communicate with other so-called "fans." Michelle Belanger founded the International Society of Vampires out of intellectual curiosity, not because she wanted to become a vampire herself.

"I made it very clear the ISV is intended to be a serious discussion of vampirism in folklore, fiction, and occultism," she said. "Thus far, most of the people who have contacted me are very serious. If they don't directly claim to be vampires—and some certainly do—they still partake of the lifestyle that goes with it. It's certain that a large number of people in the vampire subculture have a burning need to write—fiction, essays, letters, whatever, just whatever way they must to communicate through the printed word."

Real vampires also try to maintain a sense of humor about their ongoing estrangement from society as a whole. One favorite joke is, "Where can a vampire always go for compassion and understanding?"

The answer is, "A dictionary."

"Isn't it inevitable that these people are so anxious to write to each other, read about each other, get the sense that they are, actually, part of some community?" Riccardo asked. "For most, a significant moment in their lives is when they learn that, as blood-drinkers or vampires or whatever they choose to call themselves, they are not alone. There are others."

Which leads to the obvious question—how many others?

No one knows. Riccardo's conservative guess is "hundreds all around the United States. Those are just the ones who've been open about it at least in some limited way, writing to me or to others whose addresses they've gotten from publications. I myself have been in touch with over fifty, by which I mean them writing or talking to me and explaining what's been going on with them. So how many more must there be who have never tried to communicate about it with someone else?"

Michelle Belanger said one of her surveys distributed to *Shadowdance* subscribers got 125 replies from avowed vampires.

"There are all sorts out there," she said. "I was just contacted by a vampire group in Oregon requesting information. There are vampires in central Pennsylvania headed by Alexandra Long, also known as Lady Amoura. She quit to go to graduate school, but they had this very involved spirituality that vampires were a race descended from people who'd come from the stars."

Liriel said she had personally been in contact with "nine or ten people who thought they were vampires."

Dark Rose said simply, "There's no telling. But with every new issue of my *Journal*, I hear from more and more of them. They're not always the kind of people you'd expect. I have this one friend in Pennsylvania who practices blood-drinking and taking lifeforce, which to him is more important than the blood-drinking. He sleeps in a coffin and all that stuff, and by day he's a psychiatrist. Actually, I know two psychiatrists who are vampires."

There was general agreement that vampires and vampirism are here to stay.

"It's been around as long as humanity has," Michelle Belanger noted. "Popular aspects have changed now and then. They will again. Fifty years from now you'll have another generation who've embraced the concept of vampirism and tried to take it the next step forward, whatever that might be. Maybe they'll have invented cybernetic fangs."

But no matter what appearances or lifestyles are adopted by future generations of real vampires, Riccardo predicted they will always remain a mistrusted minority.

"The idea of drinking blood is always going to be a tremendous social taboo," he said simply. "Those who, for whatever reason, indulge in drinking blood will have to realize they will find it very hard to ever find acceptance among other people. That's the price."

*"When he started holding my hand, his hand was cold. I thought, 'This man is like a corpse'.... The next morning before dawn he said, 'I've got to go, the sun is coming up.' I got up and went into the bathroom. I saw my entire right inner thigh was black and blue and had these two teeth marks."*

CHRISTINE DARQUE, DESCRIBING THE
NIGHT SHE MET CHRISTOPHER

# 9
## Christine Darque

It was, right up to the moment she went into the bathroom and saw what had happened to her, a fairly typical evening in the life of twenty-two-year-old Christine. She'd recently gotten out of the army, had broken up with a short-term boyfriend, and was prowling the blues bars in her adopted hometown of Indianapolis.

That night, Christine heard that a band featuring Rod, her former guitar teacher, would be playing at a club called The Enterprise. When she got there, the band was playing as advertised, but Rod had left it two years earlier. Disgusted, she started to leave, but a strange, incredibly charismatic man asked her to join him at his table and later invited himself back to her apartment.

"I don't care what anybody else thinks," Christine said six years later as she nervously began to tell her story. "All I know is what happened to me, what Christopher did to me. I'll tell it, and anybody who doesn't believe me can go to hell. Once I might not have believed it myself. Screw this 'There are no vampires' stuff."

These days, Christine sleeps in a coffin. She's had fangs made of resin permanently attached to her teeth by an Indianapolis dentist, who agreed to her strange request. If she pulls back her lips in a snarl that bares those fangs, Christine looks scary. Otherwise, she appears completely normal, a tiny, slender woman with short hair she has dyed jet-black instead of its natural blonde.

And though in almost every other way she mimics vampire behavior, Christine doesn't drink blood. Instead, she describes herself as a vampire victim.

Christine spends lots of time corresponding with others who she says are either fellow vampire victims or else practicing or wannabe vampires.

"Sometimes it's a goddamned lousy life," Christine grumbled, lighting a cigarette, lounging back on her blood-red couch and swinging her legs up to rest her feet on a coffin she uses as a sort of coffee table/credenza. "But I've got to know a lot more. How many other Christophers are out there? How have other victims been approached?"

These days, she calls herself Christine Darque. Christine is her real middle name. "Darque" was chosen as an appropriate vampire affectation.

Her current job is answering complaint letters for a nationally famous, Indianapolis-based company that offers "eleven CDs for the price of one" deals through ads in music magazines. Fangs and all, Christine goes to work every day and writes her business letters, then spends lunch hours on her vampire correspondence.

"I eat lunch every day with two co-workers, a seventy-year-old man and a sixty-seven-year-old woman," she said. "They know I have pen pals because I sit there with them eating lunch and writing. But they don't know why I have them. I guess this vampire thing is part of me now."

Unlike many other members of the vampire underground we interviewed, Christine doesn't come from the kind of troubled background or broken home that would have made it almost inevitable for her be attracted to extreme behavior. After starting off with a few cracks about being "born a poor black child in the deep, deep South," Christine admitted almost ruefully she came from a traditional Midwestern family.

"I was born in Terre Haute, Indiana, in 1968," she said. "My dad is a welder; he can make all kinds of things—knives, tomahawks, stuff like that. My mom was a bank teller. I have a brother, he's a few years older than me. He's a welder, too. I grew up with my family in Rockville, which is about ninety minutes from Indianapolis. I guess it was all normal."

As a kid, Christine recalled, "I was a pencil-necked geek. I had glasses and pimples and was in the school band. I hung out with the geeks. That was my crowd until my senior year. That's when people started to go, 'Hey, she's okay, she plays guitar.'"

From seventh grade on, Christine took guitar lessons from two different teachers: Johnny, who showed her "every Beatles song known to man," and Rod, who taught her "heavy metal and classical—that's still my show-off stuff."

Her love for playing guitar kept Christine on the straight and narrow all through high school. She knew if she got bad grades or was suspended for being in any other kind of trouble, her loving but strict parents would take away her music lessons.

After high school, Christine moved on to Indiana State University in Terre Haute, planning to major in radio-television-film. She lived in a dormitory on campus.

"This one girl living in the same dorm thought she was a vampire, and everybody laughed at her every day," Christine recalled. "Then she went home for Christmas break, and when she came back she wasn't a vampire anymore. She stopped wearing black clothes. It was just all over for her, instantly."

Christine herself never had any interest in vampires or vampirism.

"All that stuff didn't interest me in the slightest," she declared. "I saw the movie *The Lost Boys*, and I liked it, but I wasn't compelled to do anything by it."

Though Christine didn't have the vampire bug yet, she did find herself rebelling against her solid, church-influenced background. First came a tattoo. She had wanted one badly for a long time, since her favorite musician, Brian Setzer of the Stray Cats, was covered with them.

"First I got a guitar with wings on my chest so my mom wouldn't see it," Christine said, chuckling. "My mom is so conservative. I was nineteen and extremely unhappy nobody could see my new tattoo. So I went around flashing everybody my boob. A couple months later, I went back and got one on my shoulder—a Stray Cats logo, high up on my arm so I could still wear short sleeves, and my parents wouldn't know."

Soon Christine gave her parents something worse than a tattoo to worry about. After her first year of college, she dropped out to marry Dan, the younger brother of her tattoo artist.

"I was just going to live with him for the summer, but I felt like I had to go to my parents' house and ask their permission," she confessed. "My dad said, 'There'll be no shacking up,' and Dan asked if I'd marry him, so I did. Idiot! I think hormones just took over and forced me into stupidity. If somebody stuck my ex-husband in front of me now, there's no way I'd even think about going out with him. He was a biker, really a Neanderthal and dumb and uneducated. We lasted three months, and I knew it was over."

Christine moved home for a while, but she and her parents had trouble getting along. Her father had put in a hot tub, and, Christine laughed, "I couldn't find a bathing suit with long sleeves. When my mother saw the tattoo she said the f-word for the first time in her life. She's only said it again once, when I got the fangs."

After her divorce, Christine's parents wouldn't pay to send her back to college. She lounged around their house watching television until one day her father came home from work and confronted her.

"He said, 'Do you do this every day? You're not going to amount to shit.' And when I said, 'Yeah,' he blew a fuse and knocked me out of my chair. That was the only time my dad ever hit me. So I went crying and running to an army recruiter's office and signed up. It had been in the back of my mind because one of my guitar teachers had been in the army and had told me how great it was."

The modern army offers its recruits a choice of careers. Christine wanted to go into broadcasting, but there weren't any openings. Instead, she was assigned to a journalism division and eventually stationed close to Indianapolis.

"I didn't get to do jack," she complained. "The heaviest thing I did was write an article for the local paper in Rockville saying why I joined the army. I actually wrote about my dad being so proud about it he cried. It was cornball stuff, promotional crap to get people to enlist."

Bored, Christine spent most of her off-duty time hanging out at Indianapolis coffee bars and nightclubs. Eventually she met John, whom she described as "a New Age hippie guy. He used to hypnotize people into not smoking, hypnotherapy and stuff like that. It was just amazing how he could talk people into stuff."

Suddenly, Christine wanted to get out of the army. Her tour of duty wasn't up, but that didn't stop her.

"I spent my twenty-first birthday in my commanding officer's office," she said. "He was like, 'Well, maybe you're not the kind of soldier we're looking for,' and I was like, 'Damn straight, sign the papers.'"

He did, and John and Christine set up housekeeping in Indianapolis. She got a job as a cook at a bar called the Alley Cat and soon got in the habit of drinking too much to suit her new live-in boyfriend. Three months after they'd gotten together, John and Christine split up. She was devastated and began spending nights at other bars, drinking much more than she should have. Without John, Christine felt very lonely.

"This is where the weird shit comes in," she said mournfully, lighting another cigarette and grimacing at the memory, a facial expression that inadvertently bared her long, pointed fangs. "See, I didn't know anybody, really. I always had friends, but Rockville's an hour and a half west, and that's a long drive. Anyway, one night I picked up a paper that tells what bands are playing where, and right there is a big spread about my guitar teacher's band playing a place I hadn't been before called The Enterprise. I hadn't seen Rod in six years. I flipped."

Christine headed for The Enterprise with romance in mind.

"I was dressed to kill, fishnet stockings and a leather miniskirt and all that happy jazz because I had the biggest crush on Rod in the universe," she sighed. "I looked at the stage and there's the band playing, but Rod's not with them. I walked over to the sound man and said, 'What happened to Rod?' and he slapped me on the arm and said, 'He's giving lessons in Toledo.' So there I was, standing there."

Disgusted, Christine whirled around to stalk away. But other listeners were pressing up close to the stage, and someone shoved her hard enough to make her back into a nearby table.

"I turned around to apologize to whoever was sitting there, and this is when I laid eyes on the strangest-looking son of a bitch I'd ever seen in my life," she said. "He was white as a sheet of paper, with jingling bracelets all over his arms and with long black hair basically covering everything on his face but his lips, sort of the Joey Ramone look. I said, 'You look like Joey Ramone.' He said, 'That's a new one. Sit down.' This was Christopher."

Christopher wasn't alone at the table. A beefy fellow named Larry was with him. The two men ordered Christine a beer and began talking about music. When she said she played the guitar, Christopher replied that his band needed a guitarist.

"He started asking what kind of guitar equipment I had, what kind of musical background I had. He was extremely intelligent about it and very sincere-sounding," Christine said. "My beer finally arrived, and I didn't even take a drink of it before he said, 'It's really loud here. Can we go someplace else and talk?' So I get up and he helps me put on my coat, and Larry's coming, too, and we walk outside."

Christine paused.

"Look, I was drinking a lot in those days, but on that night I hadn't had anything, even the beer Christopher had ordered for me," she said defensively. "I was perfectly straight."

Then she resumed her story.

"I got to my car thinking they were going to follow in a different car. I got in the driver's side and somehow Christopher was just through my passenger door and got in, too. I know damn well I had locked that door. I never unlocked my passenger door ever because I never had anybody getting in my car. But he did, somehow. With Christopher, I found out this stuff happened all the time."

Christine was startled, and even more shook up when Christopher insisted they drive back to her apartment, with Larry following in a second car.

"I'd thought we'd go to a restaurant, and I said he couldn't come over to my place because I had two sort of conservative roommates. They were gay, Matthew and Sharon, a man and a woman pretending to be a couple in public. And I kept saying, 'It's really late,' and he kept saying, 'It's all right, they won't care,' in this hypnotic sort of voice. I don't know how in the hell it happened, but I took him home."

When they arrived at Christine's place, Larry surprised her by racing to open first her door and then Christopher's. Christopher told her that Larry was his bodyguard.

As Christine had expected, Matthew and Sharon weren't pleased she'd brought home company. But their reaction to Christopher surprised her. Instead of insisting he leave, they both panicked at the sight of him and fled to their bedrooms, leaving Christine, Christopher, and Larry downstairs in the living room. She and Christopher sat together on a couch; Larry perched on a chair. The conversation turned to music. After a while, Christopher reached for Christine's hand.

"His hand was cold," she remembered. "I thought, 'This man is like a corpse.' But I was still thinking things could go either way. Whenever you meet somebody in a bar, you don't know what's going to go on. I guess I was attracted to him. I think anybody would have been attracted to him. Whenever he was around, women were always dropping to their friggin' knees. It was just his presence, the way he carried himself, something about him."

Soon, Christine said, Larry the bodyguard cleared his throat and suggested that Christine and Christopher "go upstairs." She was annoyed because she hadn't decided if she wanted to sleep with Christopher.

"I stood up and told them they had to leave, and Christopher goes, 'She doesn't trust me yet,'" Christine said, hunching forward and beginning to talk faster. "And then for some reason, don't ask me what or why, I was trying to make new friends, so I was like, 'What the hell?' I grabbed Christopher by the hand and took him upstairs. I walked in my bedroom and flipped on the light, and Christopher turned right around and flipped it off. And then, well, fire explodes and passion and tornadoes."

Christine and Christopher made love for the rest of the night. Several times they were interrupted by Larry, who came into the room to make sure Christopher was all right. Christine said she really didn't care about Larry barging in.

"Christopher distracted the hell out of me," she said. "When we weren't making love, it wasn't like lying next to someone who's alive. It was like lying next to a corpse. Have you ever touched something, maybe an animal, that was dead? Christopher's body wasn't stiff, but sometimes it was like there just wasn't anything inside it. But otherwise it was great. And in the morning, just before dawn, he said, 'I've got to go. The sun's about to come up.' He wrote down his phone number on a piece of paper. Larry was asleep in a chair downstairs, so Christopher got him and they left."

Feeling a little dazed by the erotic experience, Christine went into her bathroom, sat on the toilet, and almost screamed when she looked down at her leg.

"My entire right inner thigh was black and blue and had these two teeth marks," she said. "While we were doing it, I hadn't felt anything uncomfortable or painful. For a second, I thought maybe I'd cut myself shaving, I shave all down there, but I hadn't. I wanted to call and ask him what he'd done to me, but I sat around for an hour, looking at what he'd written, looking at his handwriting, before I got up the courage. Finally, I called and a girl answered. She said, 'He's been waiting for your call.' And then he said, 'I wondered how long you were going to look at my handwriting before you called.'"

Christine panicked. It took her several minutes before she could stop making small talk and ask, "Did you bite me?" After a moment Christopher said softly, "Several times," and hung up.

"At first I didn't think he drank my blood, but later I knew he did that," Christine said. "He showed up at my place a few nights later with a bunch of people, including Dee, who was his bass player. Christopher also brought over a folder of cover tunes and said, 'Learn them.' So I was in his band. It was called Lost Angels. He might have been a vampire, but his band wasn't based on that theme. It was more the old Alice Cooper-Queensryche thing."

Soon Christine found herself part of what Christopher called his porta-party. They didn't play many club shows. Instead, they'd go somewhere and drink or just hang out and listen to Christopher talk about whatever subject interested him at that moment. Once, Christine said, Dee turned to her and teased, "You know we're vampires. You're going to have to pass some sort of initiation." But Christopher immediately told Dee to shut up, and initiation was never mentioned to her again.

Christine was disappointed to learn that Christopher lived with a girl named Lisa, a dancer. Still, she and Christopher some-times had sex when Lisa wasn't around. Christine never found puncture marks on her body again after sex, but she said a few weeks after she'd joined the porta-party Christopher did bite her again, and in a way that scared her even more than the first time.

"We were in a club, and Christopher had to leave because Larry had to get up early in the morning to do something," Christine recalled. "Christopher got up and hugged me good-bye and walked out the door. I thought, well, I'm here, and went into the bathroom to fix myself up because there might be some good-looking boys around, and I looked in the mirror, and I really freaked because I had blood running down my neck. That's when I knew he was a vampire. I hadn't felt a thing, but I had the marks. Christopher's teeth are normal, they're not at all pronounced. He wasn't at my neck long enough to have taken any blood, I think. But I had the marks. They didn't heal right away."

That night, Christine said, she had a vivid dream.

"There was this barn, it was all burned down and fallen in, beams and ashes everywhere," she shuddered. "I was crawling across the beams to get in there, and rats were crawling across my hands. I'd had pet rats, so this wasn't scary or anything. I heard fluttering overhead and imagined it was bats. I got through the barn into the middle of a clearing, and Christopher was lying there like he was dead. I went over to him and started shaking him to wake him up. He sat up, and his eyes were red, not blue like they really are, and he said, 'I am an angel of darkness,' and bit me on the neck, and it hurt like hell. In the dream, it hurt like a mother. Then I woke up because the phone was ringing. It was Christopher. I said, 'I just had this really weird dream about you,' and he said, 'I know.' He's laughing. He goes, 'Don't you like rats and bats? I admit, the barn was a little bit squalid, but what do you expect from a bad dream?' And then he hung up."

At this point, Christopher took over Christine's life. He made most of her decisions for her. One was to make her take a job as a topless dancer at a club called Bud's. She'd briefly earned money dancing topless before, when her marriage was breaking up and she needed money. Now she took up the profession full time and kept at it for several years. Apparently it wasn't something she felt especially comfortable doing—when she talked to us about it, and the subject came up several times, Christine never said the same thing twice. Sometimes she said it was fun, she enjoyed it, and other times she complained she had to drink a lot every night to get up the nerve to go onstage. But it was what Christopher told her to do. He continued to dazzle her by reading her mind or revealing he knew what she'd just dreamed.

"For a year, maybe two, it became a game for him," Christine said. "Maybe I'd dream about walking down the street with him in the rain under an umbrella, and the next day I'd see him and he'd grab my arm and say, 'Umbrella.' There weren't any more incidents with biting or blood. I never asked him about that second time because I'd accepted what he was. I thought he was a vampire. I still do. I didn't want to leave him. Since then I've done all this research. There was this woman in Pennsylvania who was a vampire victim like me, and this vampire took so much of her blood that she was hospitalized. And then there's this man in Cincinnati who had a one-night stand sort of thing where he was a victim, and what I can tell you is every victim I've met or written to has been pretty happy about it, not like, 'Oh, it was so terrible.'"

One spooky night, Christine got off work at Bud's and went out with Christopher and his pals to another bar. She sat at a table with them idly listening to their conversation and suddenly noticed that, while she could hear every word, no one was moving his lips or seeming to perform any other physical action usually involved in talking.

"I was going to say something, and Christopher grabbed me before I could," Christine recalled. "Afterward, I asked him, 'What the hell were you guys doing in there?' But he wouldn't say. And after that I never could actually hear their thoughts out loud anymore, if that's what they were doing to communicate that night or whatever the hell it was."

That same night, Christine said, the gang ended up going over to the apartment of a woman Dee had met. While those two went upstairs to make love, Christine and Christopher made do on a downstairs couch. Afterward, he fell asleep. The sun came up and began to shine through a sliding glass door. Christine realized she was going to see Christopher in sunlight for the first time. "When the light came over him, it was the freakiest thing I'd ever seen," she gasped, still shaken by the thought. "He looked kind of gray. When we left, he got all bundled up with nothing exposed but his hands. He was cursing the sun all the way home. I kept asking if he was going to be all right. He was all huddled over in my lap like he was going to get sick. That's when I understood why he liked to have a bodyguard or somebody with him, to make sure he got home before dawn and was all right."

Eventually, Christopher made it clear that he wasn't especially interested in Christine anymore, at least sexually. She was still allowed to tag along with the group sometimes. Christopher would tell her what she should and shouldn't do, even in mundane matters like whether Christine should take a quick drive out to see her parents. Once when she wanted to do that, he told her not to, she'd have an accident. She went anyway and had one. So Christine concluded that she still would follow his orders, whatever they might be.

In another year or so, Christine found a new boyfriend, a younger kid named Shannon. He was nineteen, and she was twenty-four. Shannon's family had just moved away, and he spent most of his time hanging around Christine "like a little puppy dog," she recalled. Christine still was playing guitar at occasional Lost Angels shows. Shannon was in a band, too, and he was eager to meet the lead singer in Christine's group. She warned Shannon that Christopher was a vampire. He scoffed.

"So I took him over and introduced him to Christopher," Christine said. "They spent forty-five minutes talking about music. He shook Shannon's hand, we left, and Shannon was freaking out, saying, 'He's dead! He's cold! He's a vampire!' And then Christopher called to say he wanted to see Shannon some more, and Shannon was out of my place and over there like greased lightning. Basically that was the last I saw of him. He went over there and stayed. Christopher and I started fighting over Shannon. I said, 'You stole Shannon,' and Christopher said, 'I don't know what to tell you, my dear. Shannon's loyal to me.' Then I called Christopher, and Shannon answered the phone and said he'd moved in. And then he said, 'Oh, yeah, Christopher says if he wants you to play guitar for him, he'll call you.' So not only did I lose Shannon, I couldn't be around Christopher anymore. I was afraid Christopher was going to do something to me in my dreams. I just knew he could make things very unpleasant. If he had the power to read my mind, he probably had the power to screw me off. But he didn't do anything to me personally, except stealing every boyfriend I ever got in the next three years."

Christine couldn't completely wean herself away from Christopher. She constantly phoned him. Once in a while, he'd talk to her for a few minutes.

She never stopped feeling his influence or respecting his powers. During our interview, just as Christine was describing her first night with Christopher, one of the miniature recorders we were using jammed momentarily. Christine suggested, with real concern in her voice, that Christopher was somehow listening in and had stopped the tape from recording to indicate his displeasure.

Even after she was moved out of Christopher's inner circle, Christine kept on dancing topless at Bud's. She needed income to subsidize her outside interest. Vampirism, which once held no attraction for her, had become Christine's obsession. She began wearing a black trench coat like Christopher's, and tried to find some way to make him openly admit he was a vampire.

"There was this weird little person named Max who always used to hang out at Christopher's, and he thought Christopher was a vampire, too," Christine said. "I had a video camera, and I sent Max over to Christopher's to tape him. He was supposed to say he'd gotten the camera from somebody else, not me, and that he was going around taping all of his friends. He did it. He went to Christopher's and started asking him stupid stuff, and then he finally came out and asked, 'Are you a vampire?' and Christopher got up and took the camera away from him."

Christine began reading all the books about vampirism that she could find. Rosemary Guiley's *Vampires Among Us* had some addresses of experts on the subject, and Christine wrote to Martin Riccardo in care of his Vampire Studies organization in Chicago.

"Other than the addresses, I really didn't like *Vampires Among Us*," she said. "There were people in there with all their piddly stories about how they cut their fingers and their friends' fingers with an X-ACTO knife for a snack, like it's some great bonding ritual. Meanwhile, some of us are sitting around with vampires like Christopher, and we're getting brainwashed. Christopher had a powerful hold on us."

Christine and Riccardo exchanged several letters. At her request, Riccardo passed along some addresses of others who'd written to him claiming to be the victims of vampires. Christine wrote to them all, and most replied.

"That was cool because I was finding out there were other people running around like Christopher," she said. "And then in April 1992, I got together with David A."

Christine met David A., a talented bass guitarist, in the same club where she'd once met Christopher. Though David A. wasn't a vampire, he resembled Christopher physically, including having long black hair and very pale skin.

"When we met, we spent two weeks together without parting from each other's company at all," Christine remembered. "When I went to work, he'd come to the bar with me. This was the first successful relationship I'd been able to have without Christopher getting in the way."

David A. and Christine meshed muscially, too. They made some demo tapes and hoped for a show-business break. It seemed to come when Martin Riccardo wrote to invite them to a show in Chicago called The Vampire Circus. It was being staged by Vlad, a blood-drinking friend of Riccardo's who led a rock band called The Dark Theater.

"The show was on Halloween, and the night before Marty and Vlad were both on the TV show 'Sightings,'" Christine said. "I was impressed with that. Then we went to The Vampire Circus in this huge theater, this Chicago theater, and I thought Vlad was good, but I couldn't understand the lyrics. Afterward, we met Vlad, and the first thing I asked him was, 'Who's your dentist?' His fangs were beautiful. I thought having fangs would be just the coolest thing. They had a drawing for door prizes, too, and one prize was dentist-made fangs. I didn't win. When I told Vlad he said, 'Why didn't you tell me you wanted to win them? I'd have rigged it so you did.'"

Christine and David A. were too shy to ask Vlad to listen to their demo tapes. They went back to Indianapolis, got out the phone book, and began calling dentists. Christine made David A. make the calls. He asked dozens of dentists, "Could you make me some vampire fangs?" before one finally said to come over to the office.

"Actually, Sabrina's not even a dentist, she's an assistant," Christine laughed. "The dentist just stood there. Sabrina did all the work. The fangs she made us are made of resin. It's the stuff they use to fix broken teeth. It's a cheap route to go, a couple hundred dollars. Porcelains like Vlad has are incredibly expensive."

Right away, Christine found out having fangs would require a lot of adjustments.

"You have to learn to eat all over again," she sighed. "You can't chew your food from side to side anymore. You've got to chew straight up and down, like a dog. You can't grind stuff. I had to learn to drink out of a glass all over again because I'd put my mouth over it, and my fangs would hit the rim of the glass."

Even sleeping was compromised. As Christine would nod off, her fangs would bang against her lower teeth. Every so often when that happened, one of the fangs would break.

"So I had to start using a mouthpiece when I slept," Christine said. "At first I went to a sporting goods store and got a football player's mouthpiece. Later on, Sabrina gave me a different mouthpiece, and that's the one I wear now when I'm sleeping."

Her new fangs proved to Christine that she could never, ever be a vampire herself.

"When we first got them, David A. and I played around with people, sort of putting our fangs on their arms or something and biting down gently, saying we were going to get their blood," Christine said. "We were curious to see just what those fangs were capable of doing. Then I did bite one man, but it was an accident. I was at the club dancing, and he picked me up off the floor and was spinning me around and everything, and I had my fangs up around his neck. He'd been singing this song over and over again, the one by the Righteous Brothers, 'Baby, baby, I'd get down on my knees for you,' and kept on singing it. I said if he sang it one more time I'd bite him, and he did, and we were just goofing around, being silly, and he stabbed his own damn neck on my fangs. At first I thought he must have gotten ketchup on his neck someplace, but then I saw it was blood running down, and I damn near got sick to my stomach. He threatened to sue, but, hell, he'd really done it to himself. I knew then that actual blood, seeing it, would make me sick all the time."

Fangs in place, Christine and David A. got back in touch with Vlad.

"I called Vlad's machine and told him David A. and I had a tape of our music we wanted him to hear but that we wanted to give it to him in person," she said. "He arranged for us to meet him at a party of Marty Riccardo's. We did, and Vlad was every bit as charismatic as Christopher. I thought they were almost too much alike. But Vlad is mortal, at least his body is mortal. He says his immortality is through reincarnation. Anyway, we played the tape, and I got on my bended knee right in front of Vlad and asked if he would produce us. He said, 'Yes.'"

But things with Vlad didn't work out exactly the way Christine and David A. hoped. They joined The Dark Theater, sometimes commuting three times a week by car between Indianapolis and Chicago. Mostly they worked as roadies. David A. played bass just twice onstage with Vlad. Christine said she played onstage, too, though she was vague about where and when. Vlad, contacted later in Chicago, said she was never anything but a roadie.

"She was so drunk most of the time she probably doesn't remember what she did and didn't do," he sneered. "David A. is a good guy, he's talented. Sometimes I felt like slapping him on the head and saying, 'Hey, why are you letting this girl yank you around?'"

Before David A. got his chance to play with them, The Dark Theater traveled to Louisiana to appear as an opening act for Starship, a band formerly known as The Jefferson Airplane. A booth was set up for Christine to sell The Dark Theater's various products—a CD, T-shirts, gimme caps with TDT emblems.

"We got more attention than the rest of the band because David A. and I had fangs," Christine giggled. "We had the press all over us. We were signing autographs and kissing babies."

Again, Vlad disagreed.

"What happened was, she got so drunk she didn't know what was going on, and somehow we lost two hundred dollars' worth of merchandise," he said. "Look, I don't think Christine's really a bad person or anything, but she's not anybody we were going to put in the show, you know?"

Vlad said he told Christine to get lost. She said she just got interested in doing other things. One thing was a trip to New Orleans, where she fell in love with a male stripper, and informed

David A. that they could remain roommates, but now would be just friends instead of lovers. He agreed to the new arrangement.

After the stripper went out of her life, Christine met and became engaged to Jeremy, a devout Christian. She did her best to blend her lifestyle with his, but it didn't work. She did quit dancing at the topless bar—"I just drank too much when I was at that place"—and eventually landed her current job with the record club.

While all this was happening, her fascination with vampirism grew stronger. Thanks to Riccardo's never-ending supply of addresses, Christine corresponded with similarly fixated people all over the country.

"See, Marty gets so much mail he can't possibly answer it all," she explained. "He knew I'd write back to these people, listen to what they had to say, and sometimes bring the more interesting ones to his attention."

In 1991, Christine started sleeping in a coffin. She got her first from a friend who owed her a hundred dollars in back payments for a '57 Chevy she sold him. When he built her the coffin, she forgave the hundred-dollar debt. She went to a flea market, bought a huge crucifix, and nailed it to the coffin lid. When she moved in with David A. they slept in a bed, so she used the coffin as a desk.

Christine's father wasn't thrilled with the idea, but he and Christine were getting along well enough for him to build her a tiny coffin to be used as a jewelry box. She keeps her mouthpiece in it, as well as the points of two fangs she's broken and since replaced.

Recently, Christine moved out of the apartment she shared with David A. for another place in a Northeast Indianapolis suburb. Her new town house complex is directly behind a junior high school. The town houses are all slightly seedy, with flaking paint and cracked door frames. When she moved in, Christine brought her old coffin and a new, much bigger one that became her place to sleep.

"You ought to see the looks you get from new neighbors when you move in with a couple coffins," she cackled. "And there were these neighbor kids who'd been running around knocking on peoples' doors and then running away when they opened them. I got this knock on my door and walked to it real softly, threw it open, and snarled, 'Yeah?' with my fangs sticking out. When the kids calmed down enough, one of them said real quietly, 'We'll be glad to take out your trash for you.' So the fangs really help."

Coffin-sleeping, Christine said, was an acquired skill.

"When you're going to get in for the first time, it just sits there, looking like this big freight train looming," she said. "You think, 'That's what I saw Grandma buried in last week.' But getting in a coffin really gives you a good sense of your place in the world. It's where you're going to be some day, so why not get used to it? I got used to it, but every once in a while I still wake up and think, 'Damn, I'm in a coffin!' I do leave the top half open. When it shuts, you see, it locks. Coffins do that. I had to act like Houdini and mess with the locks from the inside so that if it ever does fall shut while I'm inside, I can get out. I've practiced. If I don't panic, I can do it. But you really have to have really small fingers and just get in there and dig at it."

Later in the same afternoon, Michelle and David Belanger, publishers of several vampire magazines and newsletters, arrived at Christine's town house. They'd made the five-hour drive from Cleveland after hearing about our book project. While we were talking to them, Christine suddenly mentioned the videotape her friend Max had taken of Christopher. She asked if we wanted to see it.

Michelle stifled a giggle as the tape began to play. Max had a high, reedy, extremely annoying voice, and he asked silly questions as he stuck the camera in Christopher's face. Christopher had long, dark hair, a white shirt with puffed sleeves and cuffs, and a two-day stubble of black whiskers. He spoke softly, the way

Christine had described. He sounded slightly stoned. Most of his answers were brief. When Max asked, "Are you a vampire?" Christopher looked bored and languidly reached up to take the video camera away from him.

"He looks rather interesting," Michelle said in a tone meant to convey polite interest. We weren't the first to see the Christopher video. Apparently Christine often showed the video-tape to visitors. She'd sent a copy to Cayne in El Paso, and Cayne was so taken with Christopher that he became, along with Michael Jackson, the person she wanted most to meet.

Vlad had seen the tape, too, and in his opinion Christopher resembled "a heroin-sniffing lowlife who Charlie Manson would-n't have let into his family." When we watched it, we certainly didn't sense anything even slightly charismatic about Christopher.

But Christine was rapt as she stared at the TV screen.

"I must have watched this billions of times," she said, her eyes never leaving the flickering image of Christopher's face. Then she started telling Michelle and David the story of how she met Christopher. In a way, she said, she was lucky. Through Martin Riccardo, she'd gotten the addresses of five other "vampire vic-tims." Each said being bitten by a vampire hurt.

"I didn't feel a thing," she laughed. "I still talk to Christopher every once in a while on the phone. I have to use a voice-altering control so he won't hang up."

Christine interrupted herself to point at the screen.

"See? See that? That's the way he moves. It seems so slow, but it's really fast," she said. "Oh, Christopher. He's really, really something special."

*"Lugosi was not evolution but revolution. You go back and look at your
images of the vampire in the* Varney the Vampire *penny-dreadful
stories. You know the countenance, the rat-ape, brutal, murderous, grimacing
creature. Look at your illustrated editions of* Dracula, *and you'll see
something not unhandsome but definitely not attractive either. And then all
of a sudden with Lugosi you see a transformation to this cold, distant,
aloof, exotic but very handsome matinee idol."*

MICHAEL H. PRICE, FILM CRITIC,
*FORT WORTH* (TEXAS)
*STAR-TELEGRAM*

# 10
## *The Vampire in Movies*

Awhite, groping hand appears on the flickering screen.
Reaching up from the inside, it lifts the lid of an old,
wooden coffin, and slowly a black figure appears. Count
Dracula stares wordlessly at his wives in his first appearance in the
1931 film *Dracula*, but this is not the hairy monster Bram Stoker
imagined. Neither is it the rat-faced Count Orlock who terrified
German moviegoers nine years earlier in Nosferatu.

This Dracula is sensual, with piercing eyes and a smirk hov-
ering near his full lips. There's a sexuality to the vampire even
when he's bent double with bloodlust, as when Renfield cuts his
finger while visiting Castle Dracula. Lucy Westenra immediately
falls for him, and Mina Seward alternates between horror and
excitement after being bitten.

Bela Lugosi changed the face of vampirism for the next sixty
years. From Christopher Lee to Tom Cruise, no actor would
become an icon of vampirism like Lugosi. Since that film, vampire

representations from the silly (The Count in *Sesame Street*) to the serious (Gary Oldman in the 1992 movie *Bram Stoker's Dracula*) featured the cloaked, thickly accented Transylvanian stereotype. Not only did Lugosi (with *Dracula* writers Hamilton Dean and John Balderston) set the vampiric standard for movies, he caused a revolution in vampire literature as well.

Movies play a large role in the world of vampires.

Dark Rose regularly reviews movies in her journal, with ratings ranging from Shrug ("Ugh.") to Kiss ("Excellent. Gotta read it, gotta see it, gotta do it."). The 1967 Roman Polanski comedy *The Fearless Vampire Killers* and 1985's *Fright Night* both earn a Kiss, while a 1994 documentary called *Vampires* gets a Hug and the 1987 Anthony Perkins-Mia Sara film *Daughter of Darkness* only gets a Wink. Dark Rose's twelve favorite "dark" films, printed in issue 3, include 1922's *Nosferatu*, *Romeo and Juliet* from 1966, and 1987's *The Lost Boys*.

Liriel McMahon's *VRI News* also reviews films.

"If I wasn't writing reviews, I'd probably take in fewer movies, because I've seen a lot of bad ones," Liriel says. "Well, I did really like *Interview With the Vampire*, even though I was expecting it to be horrible. A recent film noir I saw was *Nadja*. It was a really good surreal film. There's been more I've been wanting to see, like Mel Brooks's new one, and this new one coming out by Tarantino."

Christine Darque was wearing a *Lost Boys* T-shirt the day we interviewed her. She admitted to loving the movie even before becoming obsessed with vampirism. *Lost Boys* starred teen heartthrobs Corey Haim and Corey Feldman in a witty, scary look at what happens when big-city folks move to the vampire-infested small town of Santa Clara, California. In keeping with twentieth-century tradition, beauties Keifer Sutherland and Jami Gertz played the undead, quite a change from the shambling corpses of eastern European legend.

"Lugosi was not evolution but revolution," says Michael H. Price, film critic for the *Fort Worth* (Texas) *Star-Telegram* and author of four books, including *Human Monsters: The Bizarre Psychology of Movie Villains* (1996) and *The Cinema of Adventure, Romance and Terror* (1989). "You go back and look at your images of the vampire in the *Varney the Vampire* penny-dreadful stories. You know the countenance, the rat-ape, brutal, murderous, grimacing creature. Look at your illustrated editions of *Dracula*, and you'll see something not unhandsome but definitely not attractive either. And then all of a sudden with Lugosi you see a transformation to this cold, distant, aloof, exotic but very handsome matinee idol."

Why did Dean and Balderston tamper so vastly with Stoker's creation? Money.

"Hamilton Dean and John Balderston, the great pleasers of the mass audience, envisioned doing a Dracula that would also fit the matinee idol image that was so popular on the London and New York stages," Price says. "To this end, they took Stoker's description of Dracula as gaunt and menacing—that in itself being kind of a raw sexuality, a harsh eroticism—and transplanted that predatory sexuality to what I would call the pretty-boy image. They very wisely cast a handsome, decidedly youngish middle-aged actor from Hungary named Bela Lugosi to play this reinvented vampire.

"Lugosi was very pretty in the role. The ladies went crazy about him. He had been touted by Universal Pictures (who released *Dracula*) as the male Garbo when he made his entry into talking pictures early in the Depression years."

The revolution began and ended with Lugosi, Price says. It's true. Since 1931, vampires have been beautiful creatures played by the likes of Frank Langella, Keifer Sutherland, Tom Cruise, and Brad Pitt. It's as if the film world took more from Dr. John Polidori's 1819 novella *The Vampyre* than Stoker's *Dracula*.

"[Lugosi] was the Byronic, handsome, tragic seducer," Price says. "That was a wise marketing move because you sell more tickets to see something handsome and threatening than you sell tickets to see something ugly and threatening. I would probably give Max Schreck's performance in *Nosferatu* the edge for being effective in a scary sense, but there's a suave menace to the Lugosi Dracula. It's definitely more Lord Ruthven than Dracula, and I think in the popular view Dracula has become more of that type than Stoker envisioned."

Modern movie vampires have been Lugosi clones, very romantic seducers who promise pleasure with the pain. John Carradine played Dracula in the 1940s, and was followed by Christopher Lee in the 1950s and Frank Langella in the 1970s—all sensual, handsome men. Even in the spoofs, the count has been portrayed by the oily, ever-tan George Hamilton (1979's *Love at First Bite*) and deadpan, distinguished Leslie Nielsen (1995's *Dracula—Dead and Loving It*).

A notable exception was the 1996 Quentin Tarantino/Robert Rodriguez movie *From Dusk Till Dawn*, and even that subscribed to Price's hidden menace theory. The vampires in *Dusk* looked like normal people at first but eventually morphed into hideous lizardlike creatures.

"Tarantino is coming off creature designs developed in the 1980s," Price explains. "There's a great deal of *Lair of the White Worm* in this new picture. *Lair* was a very obscure film, and today it remains so, but you can tell Tarantino saw it and took it seriously. The hideousness of those creatures (in *Dusk*) is a throwback to the heavy-effects splatter movies that John Carpenter, for example, made in the early to middle 1980s."

The difference is also in the vampires: "We're not talking about the European vampire [in *Dusk*]," Price says. "We're talking about a third-world vampire. That gives it a weird international hybrid quality, much like in 1913's *The Vampire* and in transformation films from the Philippines in the 1960s and '70s. So it's actually an apples and oranges comparison to the usual vampire films."

Yet the vampire as European seducer has dominated all forms of vampire media since 1931. Lugosi not only changed the movie image of Dracula's brood but also the whole playing field of vampire fiction. Where literature once drove film, the cinema now has control, and vampires have become erotic, appealing creatures. Whitley Streiber's 1981 book *The Hunger* follows a sexy female vampire in search of a new mate. Chelsea Quinn Yarbro's Comte de Saint-Germain, who starred in five novels and several short stories, is a genteel nobleman with impeccable manners and a penchant for wearing black.

Most obvious are Anne Rice's *Vampire Chronicles*. Lestat is the eternal French aristocrat whose sexuality makes prey not mind being bitten—a far cry from the animal creature who literally scared victims to death in James Malcolm Rymer's *Varney* tales of the 1840s. It's fitting that Lestat, Louis, and Armand were played by screen hunks Tom Cruise, Brad Pitt, and Antonio Banderas, respectively, in the 1994 film adaptation of *Interview With the Vampire*.

"I don't know that Tom Cruise is the actor of the caliber to be playing that kind of role, but he definitely fits the arrogant prettiness or the qualities of aloof arrogant handsomeness that the mass audience wants in its vampires," Price says. "The support cast in that particular film, especially when you get down to Antonio Banderas—that's more my idea of a classic Lugosi-style vampire, a little more hot-blooded maybe, a little more passionate. But still with that otherworldly, sardonic quality. That, for my money, was the scene-stealing performance in the first of what I fear will become a Lestat series."

Price says film has taken the mantle of influence from literature simply by edging out the competition: "I find it appalling that most people who claim to be fans of Gothic and supernatural horror literature really never have read the great classics of that genre because they've gotten too lazy to read. Truth is, reading Stoker's *Dracula* is a little like swimming through quicksand in some passages, but I think it's worth it.

"I don't think the printed word has influenced today's writer that much," Price continues. "There are many novels of a terrifying nature that do not read like novels so much as they read like treatments for a screenplay. Look at Ira Levin, Michael Crichton, even the Lestat books—I don't find in them the same substance that I find in Stoker. And I think that is a direct consequence of this heavier influence that the convenience of film has worked on people today who write for a living. Aside from the padding of all that purple prose, the Lestat books are not all that substantial. To defend them as serious literature, that's an insult to Wells and Stoker and Shelley and Polidori and all those people—Lovecraft and Poe, for Pete's sake—who laid the foundations for what today we who work in the idiom of Gothic and supernatural horror are trying to do. Of course, I would never deny the fun of movies, but movies should not influence literature so much as literature should influence movies. I think they've got the cart before the horse in that respect."

*"The one thing I would love for you to print is that in no way do I condone this. Because I drink blood doesn't mean you should do it. If you do, in most cases I would consider you a moron. It's probably not for you. I don't even know if it's right for me. I could be completely insane."*

VLAD

# 11
# *Vlad*

Vlad doesn't really think he's the reincarnation of the original Vlad the Impaler. That's just public relations stuff, a show-bizzy hook dreamed up a few years ago by Vlad and his agent to draw attention to The Dark Theater, Vlad's band, and its self-described "Industrial-Egyptian-Metal" music.

No, Vlad believes he's the latest incarnation of one of Vlad Tepes's henchmen. Not a nice one, either.

"The 1400s are the first thing I remember," Vlad said. "I was a torturer at the time. And that's where I learned my blood-drinking repertoire. By drinking his blood, you thought you were gaining the enemy's secrets."

Nearly six centuries later, Vlad is still drinking blood—his wife's, once a week, usually on Thursdays. He doesn't do it in hopes of acquiring vampiric superpowers. It's his contention that drinking blood results in memory somehow being permanently imprinted on the soul, so that in future incarnations he'll remember his current life just as well as he does his stint as a 1400s torturer.

"I'm not a vampire," Vlad said emphatically. "I'm a blood-drinker. I admit when the vampire image came up as a way to get my music in front of people, I took it and ran with it. The whole

point is to have fun. I like to entertain. But if anybody sees me
and listens to me and takes the vampire thing too seriously, hey,
slow down there! Me onstage is not me offstage. But I'm a blood-
drinker, and there are those who think if you drink human blood,
you're a vampire, that simple definition and no more. Too bad,
because they're missing a lot."

⚜

Whether or not he calls himself a vampire, Vlad is probably the
most famous blood-drinker in America who's not a psychopathic
killer. In the last half-dozen years, Vlad's been profiled in *USA
Today* and the *Chicago Tribune.* Sally Jessy Raphael, Joan Rivers, and
Montel Williams are among the ubiquitous TV talk show hosts
who've welcomed Vlad as a guest. Around the country, many
famous rock-and-rollers at least know about Vlad even if they
haven't heard any Dark Theater music. And in Europe, well, he's
the most famous Vlad since Tepes.

Within the underground vampire community, Vlad's
looked on as a sort of unofficial prince. Blood-drinkers we met
who'd never made Vlad's acquaintance peppered us with questions, wanting to know what he was like, what he was wearing,
everything he said.

Even Christine Darque, whose musical relationship with
Vlad hadn't gone at all smoothly, said he ranked second only to
her beloved vampire Christopher as a forceful, charming, mysterious personality.

"When I first met Vlad, I'd read about his saying his body
was mortal, and his immortality came through reincarnation,
but I really didn't buy into it," Christine said. "After meeting
him and hearing his music, I knew whatever he said was really

something to be listened to. When he starts to talk about past lives, you believe him."

Even Martin Riccardo, who may have spent time with more blood-drinkers than anyone else in the vampire research field, felt Vlad had a certain unique charisma. After spending hours telling us about many so-called vampires really being blood fetishists, explaining most blood-drinkers were lonely or kids playing dress-up, Riccardo felt compelled to add, "The thing is, Vlad is the exception to everything I've just told you."

Of course, Riccardo and Vlad are close friends. When we joined them one cold winter night in a Chicago pizza parlor, Riccardo and his wife Denise had brought along some gifts to help Vlad celebrate his 565th birthday—a bottle of Black Death vodka and a tiny jug of Jagermeister schnapps, which other vampires we'd met around the country all seemed to know was one of Vlad's favorite potations.

"Great! Great!" Vlad bellowed as he tore open his packages. Everybody in the restaurant looked at him, but he either didn't notice or didn't mind. You get used to people staring at you when you sport flowing black hair down your back, and a Mephistophelean mustache and goatee that contrasts remarkably against very pale skin. But it's also probable people would have stared at Vlad if he'd had short hair and been clean shaven. Riccardo was right. Vlad had the kind of charisma no amount of vampire fakery could ever have provided.

Then there were the fangs. Vlad's made Christine's look like the inexpensive imitations she admitted they were. Christine's fangs were waxy white and narrowed to blatantly artificial points on the end. Vlad's hung down from his incisors, too, but they had the slightly off-color tinge of normal teeth and more or less sloped to their sharp ends. Our waitress certainly noticed Vlad's fangs; it was evident by how carefully she pretended not to see them. He played up to her nervousness just a little, curling his upper lip back a bit more than necessary when ordering his beer and pizza.

On first acquaintance, Vlad had lots of things he wanted to know. Unlike most of the other blood-drinkers, he didn't tell us how flattered he felt by our request for an interview. Instead, he commenced his own interrogation. What exactly were we trying to accomplish with our book? Would we quote him exactly and not paraphrase? What kind of agreement would we make to identify him only by his four-letter stage name? Would we put all this in writing?

"I blow off most of these interview requests now," Vlad huffed, draining his first beer bottle and waving it in the air to attract the waitress for another. "Vampire, vampire, vampire. All everybody wants to know is why I think I've lived forever. I'm so freaking sick of these people who think they're vampires or that they want to be vampires."

"Freaking" was about the least-obscene word Vlad used to describe various vampire wannabes he'd met over the years. He didn't deny he had flagrantly exaggerated his own vampire persona to entice them to buy his Dark Theater CDs—"I'm a whore, but at least I admit it!" What he wanted, he said, was an end to all the ways gullible people screwed up their lives by getting too caught up in the vampire movies and books and trying to act like those mythical creatures.

But he knew how to balance his spouting off. By the time the last bite of pizza was consumed, somehow Vlad had also found out more about us than we'd ever intended to reveal. He knew about our families, their names and interests, and our own backgrounds, getting this information without ever giving the impression of prying. Vlad was one of those rare people who could dominate part of a conversation without being offensive, then smoothly switch gears and seem just as interested in everyone else as he'd wanted them to be in him.

Vlad went on for a while about vampire music festivals he'd organized, concert tours he'd played on, stupid questions he'd been asked, and musicians who'd been his influences. After a while, the waitress stopped looking quite so nervous.

✤

About noon the next day, Vlad bounded into Martin Riccardo's living room. He'd said before we flew to Chicago for the interview that he preferred not letting people know where he lived: "There are too many crazies out there. I don't want some nut coming to pound a stake into my heart."

Vlad arrived bearing gifts: Dark Theater T-shirts for us, a press kit overflowing with Xeroxed newspaper and magazine stories about him, and two copies of *Le Petit Morte*, the latest Dark Theater CD. Song titles included "Hell in the City," "Lord of Life," and "Primal Danse Erotica." When we listened to the CDs later on, the music was surprisingly varied, the tunes complex. There were a couple of loud thrash numbers, but the overall mood of the music was thoughtful, even intellectual. Subtlety was the last thing we might have expected from Vlad's music, but, as Riccardo pointed out several times that day, Vlad was impossible to categorize.

After handing out the presents, Vlad plopped onto an over-stuffed chair with the natural aplomb of a frequent guest in a good friend's home. His hair and beard looked the same as the night before, and he still wore a leather jacket and gimme cap. It took us a few minutes of quiet puzzling before we figured out what was different—his fangs were missing.

"Oh, yeah," Vlad chuckled. "I've got 'em in my pocket. They can come on or off, you see. I wore 'em last night because I always like to see how people react. You guys might have been assholes. I put on the fangs and sort of get in people's faces, and how they react shows me whether they're just buying into the vampire bullshit, or whether they really want to talk to me."

Vlad said he had become so nimble putting on or removing the fangs that he was able to remove them during meals and then get them back on without anyone noticing.

"That waitress, if she'd looked while I was eating pizza, she'd have wondered where the fangs had gone," he said. "I put them in my pocket and then got them back in my mouth after I was done eating." He reached into the pocket of his jeans and extracted a small case; opening it, he showed us the fangs, resting on a soft, velvety lining and looking for all the world like two real, extralong incisors. Grinning, Vlad used his fingertips to pick up the false fangs; he popped them into his mouth like Chiclets. A few gyrations with his tongue behind tightly compressed lips, and voila! Vlad bared his teeth, and the fangs hung menacingly in his mouth again. Demonstration over, he removed them, replaced them in the case, and put the case in his pocket.

"My wife, Lynda, was going to come this morning, but she had some family celebration come up," Vlad said as he settled back into the easy chair to begin the interview. "We're both very family-oriented. My folks are gone, but I've got lots of relatives here. I was born in Chicago. I've got a brother and sister I love a lot, too, real geniuses, both of them. I don't want you to use my real name 'cause I don't want them bothered. They've got real normal lives, and I don't want to screw with that. In lots of ways I think my own life's been real normal. Just like the Brady Bunch, I like to think of it."

No Brady kid from that venerable TV sitcom ever drank human blood, but then Vlad's childhood wasn't funny, either, despite his insistence he remembered it as mostly a happy one.

"My parents were divorced, and I moved around between Chicago and Vera Cruz, California," he said. "I'd go to California to stay with my older brother, and then I'd come back here to stay with an aunt. My mom just had to work her ass off. She was an accountant, and she had a couple of jobs at the same time trying to support three kids, put two of them through college—my brother and sister, of course, not me. They were a lot older than I was, twelve years older, thirteen, like that. But it was a good childhood. I had a great life. People always think I got to be what I am because I grew up somehow in a bad way, but I didn't. Forget that."

About the same time he started first grade, Vlad discovered he had two natural talents—music and drinking blood. Later, the combination would become his profession; at first, music took precedence.

"My advantage when I was small with much older siblings was that I'd listen to the music they liked," Vlad said. "Gladys Knight, Jefferson Airplane, Jimi Hendrix. And I got into classical music. My uncle used to like that. I absorbed musically everything that was there. I became an instant child prodigy, sort of. I could play any musical instrument you handed me. I played brass and percussion. I did have a hard time with reeds because I had an overbite. I was told right away I had the talent to play at high symphonic professional levels. Music was it for me in school. Otherwise, the school system seemed like a lot of crap. My attention span is very short; I must be entertained. So I had my music.

I knew there was this really great place called the library if there was any subject I truly wanted to learn about, and I took it from there. The problem was, I realized early on what it would take, what it would be like to be a symphonic musician. You don't make any money, and you really support yourself through giving lessons. My teacher was that way; he would slap my hands with a baton every time I screwed up, and then tell me how talented I was and how I was meant for a career like his."

While Vlad was discovering his musical talent, he was also recognizing an affinity for something else.

"Now, I was a good kid, but I was a hellion," he laughed. "I was tall, but very thin, and I was vicious. I got into fights, and I did whatever to win them. I would bite people. When I was six years old I bit a kid and got blood. His blood got in my mouth and I swallowed it. Okay, here things got really weird. Maybe I should tell you what I believe. I believe we come back after death, but I don't think it's the Buddhist stepladder to Nirvana. I think you just keep coming back, because this incredible ball of energy that animates us and allows us to talk and lets you fly here from Texas, all these marvels, I don't believe this ball of energy would just let me die, drift off into the stratosphere and get a harp and wings or anything else. I drank that kid's blood by accident, and I had this reaction. It wasn't anything like, 'I am omnipotent,' more like, 'Hey, I've done this somewhere before.' Not the biting. The blood consumption. I don't say I found it pleasurable. It was just compelling. I didn't do anything about it again until I was in my teens, but I can't say the feeling went away. It didn't make complete sense to my six-year-old mind, but when it happened it was like"—here Vlad vented a theatrical sigh—"your mom putting a blanket over you when you fall asleep on the couch. Warm. Comforting. Secure."

Vlad's second epiphany came a half-dozen years later. Not long before his twelfth birthday, he went into a music store to buy accessories for some of his symphonic musical equipment—brass polish, valve oil, mouthpieces. Then he saw *it*—an electric guitar.

"It was cherry red," he recalled in Riccardo's living room, beaming at the memory. "It was cheap, maybe sixty dollars, and the strings were so far off the neck. Well, I stood in that store, and I looked at the various symphonic instruments. I thought, 'I'm never gonna get any girls with *that*.' Then I looked at the guitar and thought, 'But if I learn to play *that*, I'm there!' I went home, and that guitar was all I talked about. I think my mother got it for my birthday, and that was it. I'd sit in my room listening to Hendrix and Iron Butterfly and Kiss and Ted Nugent and whatever bad rock was playing on the radio and try to play along. I'd use a little tape recorder so I could listen to myself afterward. That really blew school for me. The dilemma was, do I study three hours a night and get good grades, or do I practice the music? Well, what do you think?"

And so Vlad ended up quitting school for good when he was fourteen. He spent his days sleeping and his nights playing guitar with a series of hard-core punk and heavy metal bands. Utilizing the same musical talent that had made him a symphonic prodigy, Vlad would take his guitar to band auditions and blow away any competition.

"The guys I ended up playing with would look at me suspiciously and say, 'How old are you?'" he said. "I'd go, 'Ahem. Eighteen.' Then I'd sit there slamming the beers with the best of them, and we'd play the first time, and at the point they did find out how old I really was, it didn't matter to them anymore. I was one of the boys. So, that young, I'd stay out all night, I did what I wanted. It was one of those weird life situations where my mother had to move around because of her jobs, and I was staying with my aunt and uncle. I guess they thought for a while there I was a bit of a demon child. They couldn't make me go back to school. Maybe if my brother'd been around then, hey, my brother would probably have put my head through a wall. But he wasn't."

Instead, Vlad took up the life of a rock-and-roll gypsy.

"It was a lot of floating, living in the back of a truck, pissing in a bottle, no lights 'til you got where you were going, lots of hangovers, and fast food and sleazy chicks," he said.

And, for the first time, lots of blood-drinking.

"Blood-drinking only took place during sex early on because it was the only opportunity," Vlad explained. "You're in a city, here's a girl, she's hot, you go for it. This was pre-AIDS, obviously. AIDS changed everything. I was very lucky, and I plan on staying that way. To be a blood-drinker now, you have to be monogamous. I don't believe it's a sexual act. It doesn't really get me off. I've believed from that first time when I was six that blood acts as a catalyst to prolong your immortal life, that core, that ka, your center, your soul. By the intake of blood on a regular basis, you endow yourself with the ability to, in the next lifetime, retain characteristics and memory of who you were before. So, bit by bit, my memory went back to the 1400s."

Vlad loved his blood-drinking, rock-and-roll life. But he eventually tired of being in other people's bands and playing cover versions of songs other people had written.

"I'd go in with these older guys, and the bass player would play something," Vlad said. "I'd go, 'No, gimme that thing, here, look.' He'd get all pissed off, but the other guys would say, 'Play it the way you want, kid, you're better.' Mostly, though, I had a good time for a long while. It was like, hey, I'm having sex, I'm a monster, I'm an adult. And I was making money, not a lot, but that series of sideman jobs got me to the point where I could finance the equipment I needed for myself. I say I have to drink blood, but, hey, I also have to play music. If I couldn't play music, I'd be miserable. That would be gun-tasting time for me."

Until he turned twenty-three, Vlad played other people's music. Then he decided to go out on his own. He lived on the West Coast for a while, and also in Toronto, before finally moving back to Chicago. Eventually he came up with the concept of The Dark Theater, a band that would play his music and entertain in other ways at the same time.

"In the beginning, it was just me, another guy on the (synthesizer) machines, and then I had these girls called the Ghoul-Ghoul Girls who'd do fake throat slittings and tongue extractions and sex and all onstage," Vlad said. "Then that part evolved into hiring and using magicians. I just love a stage show. If you're going to go out there and entertain, give the audience something they'll never forget."

Vlad was deliberately vague about when he specifically got The Dark Theater started. We guessed when we met him that he might be in his early to mid-thirties, though, like most of the other blood-drinkers, he looked perhaps ten years younger than he probably was. Assuming The Dark Theater dated back to the early 1980s, though, it must have been in 1988 or 1989 that a conversation with his agent caused the genesis of "Vlad."

"I'd been going around in this big cockatoo haircut, big Elvis sideburns, long hair, totally corpse-gray makeup, and I wore tuxedos everywhere," he laughed. "I'd already become a firm believer in mythic proportions. My agent and I were talking one time about what I had to do next, so I could take that next step publicity-wise. Vladimir was already an old family name. To me Vlad, as a monicker, was ethnically right. When my family came to this country—I'm first generation American—they wanted us all to be Americans, man. Ah-MUR-i-kans! That was the ethic they tried to instill in us. We're all fairly pale, and blue and green eyes like mine run in our family. Plus from the time I was very small, when I was six like I told you about, I'd been thinking that I might be insane. I had these visions of things I couldn't comprehend, and somehow I understood more about agriculture than I should have or wanted to. So many weird flashes of things, but nothing completely coherent."

Anyhow, Vlad said, he and his agent thought they might as well blend Vlad's natural inclinations with the demonized reputation of Transylvania's most famous psychopath.

"Ah, I knew who Vlad Tepes was because he'd been a great leader," Vlad said. "There's a lot about Tepes that's little-known. I chose the Vlad name because I wanted to have a little fun. I thought, look, this is part of my life, this is what I do, because by then I had become a regular blood-drinker. I didn't call myself Vlad because I was a big fan of Bram Stoker and his *Dracula*. Still, I knew the fangs would be a good idea. They wound up costing over a thousand dollars. People did not have fangs in the '80s. I was considered to look very weird. And believe it or not, I was not then and am not now a big vampire fan."

Still, Vlad knew a lot of other people were big vampire fans, and they would certainly be the new target audience for The Dark Theater and its music.

"Man, I hit the streets with press kits and CDs, going around introducing myself as Vlad and letting people think what they wanted," he recalled. "It was a great story, a great myth. I mean, I was a torturer, never Tepes. But people dug it. What's funny is, a lot of things about me, well, they fit the myth. I'm a Romanian, but I'm incredibly pale-skinned. One of the Serbian legends is that any baby born with blue eyes and red hair is a vampire. Well, I was born with blue eyes and red hair. I don't have to tint my hair black anymore, it's gotten darker, but my beard is actually bright red."

Vlad and The Dark Theater experienced good times and slow ones. Sometimes, he said, he had to go back and do studio work to earn a living. Vlad said he also worked briefly in the Chicago Stock Exchange, and, during the last eight or nine years, as a freelance recording studio engineer. The Dark Theater did occasional live shows, including the two Vampire Circuses Vlad organized, but their act was costly to stage. Besides, Vlad said, he prefers working on his music in a recording studio, where he can play all the instruments and sing all the parts himself, adding the separate tracks together to form a seamless whole. There were occasional Dark Theater road trips to cities like Detroit, and the infamous festival in Louisiana where Christine Darque, brought along to work as a roadie, apparently let most of the Dark Theater merchandise get stolen.

As Vlad's fame grew, so did the made-up stories about him.

"From what I've heard about myself, I cannot tell you how many groupies I've gotten to sleep with in the last ten years, how many babies I've produced, all of these wonderful things people say I've done," he scoffed. "My response is always, 'Sounds great, I wish I could've been there.' I figure any publicity is good publicity. Say I'm a god, say I'm a dick, just spell the name right."

In actuality, Vlad said, he's almost conservative in his private life. He invited us to his home—we didn't have time to go—and said he lived in the same Chicago suburb as former Chicago Bears running back Walter Payton. He's been married for about five years to Lynda, who apparently was once a backup singer with The Dark Theater. He drinks her blood once a week, on Thursdays.

"We started the weekly blood-drinking before we were married," Vlad said. "I don't use my teeth to get the blood. Think about being bitten by a dog. It hurts. I've got sharp teeth anyway, I could take a chunk out. Besides, I don't want to cause her pain. I make a very small nick with a razor blade or a sharp knife. It's very clean if you do it right. I don't take much blood. And the blood-drinking is not in any way ritualistic."

During the interview, Vlad said we could call Lynda later and ask her about it. But when we called, she had decided not to discuss her husband's blood-drinking.

"Only once has someone drunk my blood," Vlad noted. "That was Lynda, and it was on our wedding night. I'm not uncomfortable with her doing it at all if she wants to. Of course, I've met other people since who want to do it, but I don't want to do it with them."

Sometimes, Vlad said, he feels concerned that Dark Theater fans and vampire wannabes might not be able to tell the difference between stage act and reality. He doesn't want to be the reason anyone else tries drinking blood.

"I don't know if it's natural, that's the hard thing," Vlad admitted. "The one thing I would love for you to print is that in no way do I condone this. Because I drink blood doesn't mean you should do it. If you do, in most cases I would consider you a moron. It's not for you. I don't even know if I'm right. I could be completely insane."

Vlad said he's even offended when famous TV talkshow hosts refer to him on-air as a vampire.

"My reaction to them is, 'I believe a lot of people are vampires,'" Vlad grumbled. "I tell them right there, 'Montel Williams, Sally Jessy, I don't know what you're getting on to me for. You're the ones sucking people dry. Being a leech is easy. That's what you do. Don't call me names.'"

On the other hand, Vlad also objects when people assume he's a non-blood-drinker who's only pretended to be one for some free publicity.

"Really, if I wanted to come up with a gimmick I could have come up with something else that would have gotten me in a lot less trouble and accepted a lot faster," he said. "It's one of those things where I said, 'This is what I am, and we'll see where it goes.'"

When we said good-bye to Vlad, he wished us luck with the rest of our interviews and urged us to stay in touch. He must have meant it. After a week or so he called just to say hello. Vlad was the only blood drinker we interviewed who did this.

A month after we'd met Vlad, Cayne Presley leaned forward in her El Paso bedroom and popped a videotape into her VCR. Christine Darque had mailed Cayne one of Vlad's music videos, and Cayne had watched it over and over again. Even though the heads on her VCR were dirty and the resulting images of Vlad were streaked and grainy, Cayne marveled as she watched him gyrate and sing.

"I can just tell Vlad's really something," she moaned. "I would love to meet him, to touch him. He's such a vampire!"

Somewhere in Chicago, Vlad was probably grinding his fangs in frustration.

*"For most vampire buffs, Dracula is the fiend who comes to haunt us and suck our blood at nighttime. For a few others, he is the aristocratic Transylvanian count from eastern Europe who wishes to conquer England and the rest of the world. For the Romanian nationalist, he represents the immortal hero of the race, ready to rise from his grave in defense of the fatherland...It is the essential immortality of both hero and antihero that provides a trait common to both these extreme images of Dracula and Vlad the Impaler."*

DRACULA, PRINCE OF MANY FACES
RADU R. FLORESCU AND RAYMOND T. MCNALLY

# 12

## *The Original Dracula*

Five hundred sixty-five years before we met Vlad in a Chicago pizza parlor, the true patron saint—if such a man can be called a saint—of vampirism was born.

To completely comprehend Dracula, it's necessary to understand his father, Vlad II. In February of 1431 A.D., Vlad II had been inducted into the Order of the Dragon, a Catholic religious order of knights. From then on, he was known as Vlad Dracul—Vlad the Dragon. Whether because he was born that year or because he was named for his father, Vlad II's second son was given the nickname Dracul-a, son of the Dragon. Dracula also meant "son of the Devil," but Vlad III would eventually prove himself far more devilish than his father. For clarity's sake, Vlad III will be referred to hereafter as Dracula.

Vlad II won praise as a crusader in the holy war against an invading Turkish army led by Sultan Murad. In December 1436, he defeated the Turkish forces in Tirgoviste, the capital of

Wallachia, another Romanian province. His sons—in descending order they were Mircea, Dracula, and Radu—followed their father to the capital. There they began their educations in Renaissance politics, learning court etiquette and knightly ideals.

Dracula's penchant for ruthlessness surfaced early on. In 1442, he and Radu were sent to live in Sultan Murad's Turkish court. It was mostly a goodwill gesture, because the war against the Turks had waned, and he had stung them enough to make them wary, but it still was clear proof of Vlad II's willingness, if necessary, to sacrifice his own sons for political gain. One year later, Pope Eugenius IV called for another crusade against the Turks to unite a rapidly splintering Christian church. Vlad II was called on to send tens of thousands of troops. If he did, it would violate his agreement with the Sultan, meaning his sons might be executed. Yet Vlad II did send four thousand troops under the command of Mircea, guaranteeing the anger of the sultan and, it appeared, sacrificing the lives of Dracula and Radu.

Such an outcome would have changed the face of the world. Dracula became a dark antihero for millions of vampire fans in the nineteenth and twentieth centuries, but, in his own era, he was also one of Christianity's greatest crusaders. He would repel the Turks several times, halting the advance of Islam through eastern Europe. Ironically, without him, both Christianity and vampirism would have lost a champion.

But when Vlad II sent his troops for battle against the Sultan, Dracula was still a scared boy in a foreign capital. For some reason, Dracula and Radu were spared. Exactly why has never been established, but it may have had something to do with the sultan's attraction to the young men. Radu later became romantically linked with Murad and, eventually, his son Mehmed. It's probable that Dracula also received the sultan's tender attentions, which could explain his predilection later in life for impaling his victims on stakes driven through their rectums.

Dracula stayed with Murad until 1448. His education continued in the subjects of science, logic, language, and Turkish tradition. It was interrupted when Janos Hunyadi, an Albanian adventurer with political ambitions, hatched a plan with Vladislav Danesti II, one of Vlad II's rivals for the throne of Wallachia. Vladislav coordinated a revolt by the Tirgoviste *boyars* (local political leaders), assassinating Mircea and forcing Vlad II to flee. He was caught and killed, and his body has never been found.

Murad released Dracula, next in line for the throne, to assume his princely duties. Armed with Turkish cavalry and Danubian infantry, Dracula briefly took control of Wallachia. But then Murad decided the war had cost him enough and declined to send additional troops. Vladislav Danesti II ousted the would-be prince, who fled back to Murad's court, then on to Moldavia.

In 1452, Dracula joined forces with his old enemy, Hunyadi, against the Turks. It seems odd that a prince should ally with and eventually befriend the man who engineered his father's assassination, but such was Renaissance politics. Vlad II himself had played both sides of the Catholic-Turkish conflict. Now Hunyadi passed on his knowledge to an intelligent protégé regarded as an up-and-coming political force.

Dracula's skills were sorely needed. Mehmed had taken over the Turkish throne when his father died in 1451, and had already proved himself a worthy successor by conquering Constantinople. Mehmed copied the tactics of Mircea, the first Romanian to use cannon in battle, by constructing a giant cannon that fired six-hundred-pound balls. These simply pulverized Constantinople's city walls.

The victory placed Mehmed on the Transylvanian border, and Hunyadi knew the Turks would come for Belgrade next. The city was on the northern shore of the Danube River, and its fall would mean Turkish ships could go straight from the Black Sea to the eastern shore of the Italian boot—a short overland distance from Rome and the heart of Christianity.

Luckily for Hunyadi, a monk named John of Capistrano gathered a force of eight thousand peasants for an unofficial crusade. When the Turks attacked in 1456, Hunyadi and John defeated a force many times their numerical superior. Belgrade was saved. But then God or nature or sheer bad luck did what Mehmed could not: A plague swept through the land in the summer of 1456, killing both John of Capistrano and Janos Hunyadi. The White Knight of Christianity was felled, but the man who would become vampirism's dark lord was coming into power.

Dracula had been sent by Hunyadi to discourage the army of Vladislav Danesti II—the old rival of Vlad II, Dracula's father—from helping Mehmed during the battle of 1456. This signified the final split between Dracula and the Turks. The prince's forces met Danesti's near Tirgoviste, where Mircea and Vlad II had been killed by Danesti, and the son of the Dragon avenged his father in hand-to-hand combat. Dracula now ruled Wallachia.

At age twenty-five, Dracula was tall and slender, with large green eyes, a long, thin nose, full lips, and bushy, dark red hair. His title alone seemed more than enough to weigh him down: "Prince Vlad, son of Vlad the Great, sovereign and ruler of Ungro-Wallachia and the duchies of Amlas and Fagaras." Dracula soon proved an able leader. He immediately established good relations with the Hungarian king Ladislas V, Janos's son Laszlo Hunyadi (then governor of Belgrade and commander of the Transylvanian army) and the mayors of Brasov and Sibiu.

The Turks became worried and sent emissaries to Tirgoviste. They asked Dracula for an annual tribute of two thousand gold ducats and, more important, free passage for Turkish forces through the region. In exchange, Wallachia would become a Turkish ally. Dracula agreed.

Turning to internal politics, Dracula saw that the *boyars* held a great deal of power in local circles, and so worked to shift their influence toward a central government. Their private armies were eventually consolidated into Dracula's forces. Dracula gave the lands confiscated from disloyal noblemen to new property-holders (usually lower-class citizens), rather than to the original nobleman's family. This created a new class of landholders loyal only to Dracula himself. He also gathered less-principled men to be *armasi,* a private police force who carried out Dracula's peculiar, bloody brand of justice.

A rebellious *boyar* named Albu Taxaba may have had the honor of becoming Dracula's first impalee. Taxaba and his army revolted just after the prince took power. Dracula overwhelmed and captured Taxaba and then rounded up his family, too. All were impaled except a younger brother who escaped.

In the spring of 1457, Dracula discovered the identity of one of his brother's murderers. Mircea had met a gruesome end, buried alive facedown so that he slowly suffocated. His younger brother invited to Easter dinner over two hundred *boyars* and others guilty in plotting Mircea's death, as well as their wives and children. When they had gathered, Dracula surrounded them with troops. The young were forced to work on building Castle Dracula, a fortress in the Arges mountains— they formed a human chain up through the mountains, passing up building materials and supplies. The old were impaled outside the Tirgoviste city walls. After that, Dracula was given the nickname Tepes, "the Impaler."

The prince became widely known for cruelty. Legends abound; it's impossible to know which are apocryphal.

One story relates how a group of Italian ambassadors refused to remove their skullcaps when addressing the prince, saying they would not remove them even for the Turkish sultan or the Christian emperor. Dracula agreed it was admirable to follow the custom with such depth of devotion, and in order to strengthen it, the skullcaps were immediately nailed to the ambassadors' heads. In other versions of the legend, the ambassadors are Turkish, and refuse to remove their turbans.

There's also the tale of the hardworking peasant wearing an old, worn tunic who was spotted by the prince. "Why," Dracula asked, "doesn't your tunic cover your legs?" The peasant replied that his wife preferred to sit at home being lazy instead of mending his old tunic or sewing him a new one. Dracula ordered the woman impaled and a new wife brought to the peasant. He made sure the man's second wife watched the first's death, so, no doubt, she afterward was always eager to sew for her husband.

Another legend concerns Dracula's policy toward the homeless. On one day, all of the beggars and homeless the *armasi* could find were gathered in a banquet hall for a huge feast. They ate and drank all day, with the *armasi* encouraging them to sleep where they fell rather than leaving once sated. Then Dracula's henchmen set the hall afire, killing everyone inside. Dracula regarded beggars as worse than thieves, who at least worked for their money.

Dracula did hate thieves, though. One foreign merchant, a story goes, came to him and claimed someone had stolen a large sum of money from him during the night. Dracula told his men to sneak money back into the merchant's cart, but with one extra gold piece included. The merchant soon returned to the prince and confessed his amazement at finding his money returned, with one ducat extra. Dracula knew then that the merchant was honest, and so let him live. The thief was found and impaled.

The prince also had a strong sense of personal pride bordering on arrogance. One tale relates his discussion with two monks. Dracula showed them a courtyard in Tirgoviste, which by then had become a forest of wooden stakes, most of them occupied. One monk expressed his disapproval on moral grounds. He was impaled. The second wisely told Dracula, "You are appointed by God to punish evildoers." He was spared.

Dracula's deep faith in Christianity never was allowed to interfere with his love of torture. The Catholic Church held strong to the belief that good works offset evil, and so the prince actively promoted the building of monasteries and was often in the company of monks. He truly believed his cruelty was atoned for in this way.

Impaling was a horrible death, however. The impaling stakes were rounded rather than sharp, so death wasn't immediate. Victims were impaled in a number of places, including the buttocks, chest, and stomach. The prince also favored a number of lesser, more conventional tortures involving mutilation.

Tales of the real Dracula's blood-drinking are few and far between. He didn't become the most famous vampire in the world until 1897, with the publication of Bram Stoker's *Dracula*. Even then, Stoker originally called his villain "Lord Wampyr." Four or five months after starting the book, Stoker stumbled across a history of Wallachia. Enchanted by tales of Dracula, Stoker renamed his antagonist for the Wallachian prince.

❦

In 1457, Dracula found himself at war with Germany. Laszlo Hunyadi had invited Hapsburg king Ladislas V to tour

Belgrade. Hunyadi knew the king would be accompanied by a certain count who was a rival of the Hunyadi family. After the king and count had crossed the drawbridge into the city, Hunyadi ordered it raised, trapping the German troops outside. The count was killed, though Ladislas was set free—Hunyadi had no quarrel with him.

Ladislas was vengeful, though, and ordered Hunyadi tried and executed. Hunyadi's brother-in-law, Mihaly Szilagy, appealed to Dracula to avenge his death. The war began in the shadows, with towns revolting, and one of Dracula's generals pledging allegiance to the Turkish sultan. Danciul, the "Old Pretender," brother of Dracula's long-dead rival Vladislav Danesti II, gave himself the title of prince of Wallachia. Vlad the Monk, Dracula's half brother, also declared himself Dracula's rival for the throne.

In 1458, Dracula led a cavalry force and began wreaking havoc, destroying German villages that supported Vlad the Monk. He then savaged the followers of Danciul. Dracula sent word that loyal merchants should flee Transylvania for Wallachia, and then he robbed (and often impaled) as many German merchants as he could find. Ladislas V died suddenly in December 1457, and Szilagy's nephew Matthias took the throne, ending the war and appointing Szilagy to mediate the dispute between the kingdom and Dracula. Hostilities ended in November 1458.

Dracula's quest for vengeance led him back into Transylvania to hunt Danciul. His bloodlust grew, as did the number of stakes foresting the landscape. In 1460, Danciul convinced the Turks that Dracula was a threat. The Old Pretender then went on the offensive, but his invasion force only got as far as the border. Dancius was captured, forced to dig his own grave and beheaded. *Boyars* loyal to the Danesti clan were impaled. A treaty was signed with their successors in late 1460, and Dracula returned his attention to the Turkish sultan.

Pope Pius II declared a three-year crusade against the Turks that year, but Dracula was the only European leader who totally favored it. Sultan Mehmed responded by conquering Serbia, putting him squarely on Wallachia's southern border. Szilagy—a man Dracula considered a brother—was captured and killed by the sultan, further angering the Transylvanian prince.

Mehmed sent a diplomat to Tirgoviste in late 1461, presumably to temporarily govern Wallachia so Dracula could travel to a meeting with the sultan at Constantinople. The diplomat was instead taken prisoner, as was another Turkish envoy who'd planned to ambush Dracula on the road to Constantinople. Then the prince organized small groups of warriors to wage almost a guerrilla war against Turkish cities. They first destroyed those towns that might have been used as bases for the Turks to cross the Danube River. Then they marched captured Turkish troops back to Tirgoviste, where they were impaled alongside the two treacherous diplomats.

Mehmed sent his best general, Mahmud, to capture Wallachia's largest Danube port. Mahmud took the city and used it to mount raids into Dracula's territories. When the prince heard the news, he attacked and cut down two-thirds of Mahmud's army. This angered the sultan to the point of declaring an all-out war. In 1462, he and his army left Constantinople for Wallachia.

Mehmed pushed his way across the Danube. Dracula preceded him back across Wallachia, destroying any food sources and slowly starving the sultan's pursuing army as well as poisoning any potential sources of water for the invading Turks. A turning point came when Dracula and his men infiltrated the Sultan's army one night and massacred as many of the enemy as they could before daybreak. That sapped the sultan's troops' religious fanaticism. When the Turks finally reached Tirgoviste and saw the forest of rotting impaled bodies there, they beat an immediate retreat.

However, Mehmed wasn't finished. He dispatched Radu, Dracula's younger brother, to appeal to the Wallachian *boyars*, who, although appointed by Dracula, were quickly becoming disgusted by his growing cruelty. Radu promised them independence from the Turks as well as relief from their prince's heavy-handed rule.

The Turkish army pushed forward again, and Dracula finally had to take refuge in his castle in the Carpathian Mountains. The Turks used cannon to lay siege to it and might have ended Dracula's life there, if not for a spy among them. This Romanian spy, a master archer, tied a warning to the end of an arrow and shot it through a window of Dracula's castle. Dracula's mistress retrieved the message and shared news of the coming assault with her lover. Then, fearing all in the castle would be killed by the Turks, she threw herself from a tower into the river below, an act that inspired the opening scene for the movie *Bram Stoker's Dracula* over five hundred years later.

Dracula, meanwhile, escaped through a secret passage and waited at a small fortress nearby for the Hungarian army of King Matthias. The two finally joined forces in November 1462. But Matthias had his own problems at home, so he soon signed a treaty with Mehmed and headed back to Hungary. But first he did what no one had accomplished before: He captured Dracula.

Matthias's strategy in taking Dracula was impressive. While traveling through the Fagaras Mountains, Dracula's troops had to be lowered by pulley to a valley below. As Dracula waited his own turn on the heights, the rest of his army was lowered. Then the Hungarians surged around Dracula and took him prisoner. They hauled the prince to a nearby fortress called Konigstein. Legend has it that even in jail Dracula captured what mice and birds he could and impaled them on bits of wood.

Dracula eventually was freed from prison after he converted from Orthodoxy to mainstream Roman Catholicism. He married Ilona Szilagy, Mihaly's daughter, and settled in Pesth (later part of Budapest). He joined Matthias's army in the liberation of Bosnia in 1476, and then turned his attention to regaining the Wallachian throne. By November of that year, Dracula was once again prince of his own home country.

Two months later, his body—*sans* head—was found in a bog near the city. His death at age forty-five has never been explained. Some say he was accidentally struck down by his own men in battle with the Turks. Other stories say it was the Turks who finally caught up with their old nemesis. Whatever the truth, the grave of Dracula—like that of his father Vlad II before him—has never been found.

*"Actually drinking blood is this sexual, erotic thing. . . You become this animal, this entity. You can let down all the barriers society has put on you, all the things you're supposed to think, all the ways you're supposed to behave. At the moment that I take someone's blood, I totally feel like a Dark Angel."*

DARK ROSE

# 13
## *Dark Rose*

Vlad is an unofficial prince among blood-drinkers, and Dark Rose may eventually become their queen by acclamation. In the winter of 1995 and the early months of 1996, her *Dark Rose Journal* had become, after just a few issues, a sensation in the underground vampire community. The contents of the journal were 99 percent erotic, but, for the other vampires and vampire scholars we met, that was only part of its charm. Dark Rose's unabashed embracing of her own bisexuality, her "in-your-face" editorial retorts to anyone who might be offended by her lusty, if somewhat fictionalized, lifestyle, and, above all, her easy acceptance of her vampirism, were a palpable step up from the well-meaning but frequently clumsy stories and essays in other vampire community publications. Besides those stories attributed to its namesake, *The Dark Rose Journal* also included excellently written contributions from subscribers using pen names like Bobbiejo and Countess Crystal Puskaric.

"The first issues of *The Dark Rose Journal* have really been impressive," said Michelle Belanger, whose own various Shadowfox publications are themselves quite well-written and insightful. "Sometimes you find people who may dress up in capes but aren't really cheesy and goofy. These people, like Dark Rose, form a very complex spirituality. Reincarnationism, from things Dark Rose has written, plays a big part in this, and, if not occultism, then neopaganism."

Even Martin Riccardo, who had so far only gotten to know Dark Rose through correspondence, said he was anxious to make her acquaintance.

"You've met her in person? What's she like?" he bubbled. "She appears to have the kind of forceful personality that can make a real difference in the way vampirism is perceived."

Along with these reactions from vampiric scholars who weren't often so deeply impressed, before we actually met Dark Rose we also had a letter from her and the latest issue of her journal. The letter, more accurately described as a short note, arrived a week before we flew to Orlando to meet her. Even the letterhead was striking. Its logo, a woman garbed in a formal gown with graceful black bat wings extending from her shoulders, was much more sophisticated than the usual fangs-and-blood imagery of the vampire underground. There was even a motto: "Enjoy the dark pleasures."

Dark Rose wrote that she hoped her letter found us doing well. If we had any questions, we shouldn't hesitate to contact her at our convenience. She was looking forward to our meeting. Until then, she wished us and our loved ones "many dark and beautiful blessings."

Then there was her picture in the *Journal*. Crouched on hands and knees facing the camera, Dark Rose flaunted strikingly beautiful facial features, a profusion of long, dangling dark hair, and the kind of cleavage seldom seen outside a teenage boy's wildest fantasies. If Dark Rose's erotic vampire essays and short stories couldn't sell her journal, then she certainly had more than sufficient physical attributes to fall back on as marketing tools.

So, apparently, this emerging vampire superstar combined intellect, moral conviction, and drop-dead good looks. It was possible, of course, that in person she was a wrinkled crone or a canny marketeer, or both, faking the whole persona to make a buck. One of her sales come-ons in an early *Journal* page coaxed, "Come to me…when you're lonely. Come to me…when you're restless. Come to me…when you need something new."

We were coming to Dark Rose with no real idea of what to expect.

Dark Rose suggested we meet for dinner at an Olive Garden restaurant near her home in an Orlando suburb. It might have been a coincidence, but other vampires we interviewed wanted to meet at various Olive Gardens, too. Michelle Belanger said one vampire group in Cleveland suggested to the manager of their local Olive Garden that blood-drinkers receive a discount as his most frequent customers.

We were supposed to meet Dark Rose at 6:00 P.M. She told us over the phone that she'd be bringing a friend along, a wise precaution for any woman meeting two men she didn't know. Since people in Florida like to eat dinner early, we arrived at the restaurant thirty minutes ahead of time to get a table. We told Dark Rose to ask for us when she and her friend arrived.

When they did, we were amazed. Not because of Dark Rose's companion, Avery—he proved to be a stocky fellow in his late forties whom she introduced as her fiancé—and not because Dark Rose herself looked so memorable. Actually, she did, but in an unexpected way. After reading her journal and seeing her photograph, we'd anticipated the presence of some dusky, exotic beauty in high heels and low neckline. In person, Dark Rose was certainly pretty, but she didn't radiate any sense of sexually sophisticated menace. Instead, she seemed for all the world like a sweet, even innocent, teenager. Her makeup was minimal; she wore a white sweater and blue jeans. Taken together, she and Avery might have been a father and a high school senior stopping at the Olive Garden for a quick dinner before going on to the movies as part of a fun dad-daughter evening. This was the vampire queen?

Dark Rose introduced herself to us using her real name, which we promised to keep confidential. It was an ordinary, pretty name. Small talk ensued, and when dinner was ordered, she politely asked for salad and soup, explaining to us in a soft voice that she mostly confined her diet to vegetables. It was a relief to have dinner with a blood-drinker who didn't scare the server.

Avery dominated most of the conversation. A pleasant sort, he told us he was a freelance writer who often developed musical programs for famous theme parks. Avery explained frankly that he and Dark Rose were, in fact, the sole writers of all journal material that had been published so far.

"We're hoping as we get more subscribers that some of the things they submit will be good enough to include," he said. "Right now we're just trying to create a certain atmosphere." Avery went on to discuss his and Dark Rose's hopes for eventually changing the modestly printed Journal into glossy magazine format. There was a market, he said, for really provocative material that appealed to readers' secret desires.

While Avery chatted, Dark Rose methodically took a series of small bites from her salad bowl and a few tiny sips of soup. Then she sat quietly, occasionally smiling or nodding when Avery mentioned some specific goal they had for the journal.

"We're quite a team," he said at one point.

Dark Rose did join in the conversation when the subject turned to reincarnation. She gave a lengthy description of her relationship with Avery in a previous life. Frequently, she said, she dreamed about being a child trapped in a burning house. A friend tries unsuccessfully to save her. Dark Rose explained she interprets the dream as a memory of an earlier incarnation, and that the friend must have been Avery.

"So even then he was someone who wanted to help me," she said.

After another thirty minutes, we suggested it would be good to set an interview time for the next day at Dark Rose's home. One P.M. was our suggestion. We'd learned over the past months that vampires were, as expected, not early risers.

"One P.M. would be fine," Dark Rose said.

"Come on," Avery scoffed. "You? Up at one?"

"I can get up," she said, the tiniest trace of steel creeping into her previously docile tone. "Be there at one," she told us again.

The four of us walked out of the restaurant, Dark Rose in front. She walked with her hands clasped behind her, the backs of her hands resting gently at the small of her back—a little girl's posture, the kind popularized by those ceramic figurines grandmothers like to display in their living rooms.

On our drive back to the hotel, we speculated that Avery might be the brains behind it all.

❦

Dark Rose lived in a pleasant, middle-class neighborhood about fifteen minutes' drive from downtown Orlando. Her directions were easy to follow, and soon brought us to a block of brick houses with large, fenced yards. Dark Rose's house differed from that of the neighbors only by the length of uncut grass. Apparently, Avery wasn't handy with a lawn mower. A child's pink bike lay across the sidewalk. The curtains were pulled shut. Across the street, cars were lined up outside another house. People dressed in somber-looking suits were gathered around the front door.

Dark Rose answered her door when we knocked and looked over our shoulders at the crowd across the street.

"That woman must have died," she called to Avery, and waved tentatively to someone at the other house as she ushered us inside.

Dark Rose escorted us to her living room; the furnishings and decorations were a strange mix of Disney and Dracula. Children's coloring books were piled alongside tomes about magic and vampirism. There were shelves full of videocassettes, again mingling children's titles with grown-ups' films. These were mostly classic films; no X-rated titles were evident. Framed pictures celebrated some of Avery's theme-park projects. Dark Rose's vampire lifestyle was represented with portraits of various movie vampires. As a sort of crowning glory, the two photographic centerpieces were portraits of Dark Rose in full Vampirella regalia. She saw us looking and laughed, "Cleavage shots."

The living room connected to another large room that served as headquarters for *The Dark Rose Journal.* Avery was sitting in front of a computer, editing an article.

"Do you want me to come in now, or later?" he asked, and he wasn't asking us.

"Later," Dark Rose said. "If the kids come in, see if they've eaten." She gestured for us to sit down, and perched herself on a long couch across from our chairs. She was wearing blue jeans again and a light-colored sweatshirt. There was a small mole on the upper corner of her mouth that we hadn't noticed the previous evening.

"I got out some photo albums if you want to see pictures of me growing up," Dark Rose began. She picked up one of the albums and began flipping through it. "That's me there, in fourth grade. And here I am in fifth, I think, at this girl's birthday party. She had a swimming pool, and everyone in class was invited to go swimming. I guess you can see something pretty obvious."

In the photos, a dozen little eleven- and twelve-year-old girls are congregated around a medium-sized pool. The kids are wearing the usual fifth-grade-girl swimsuits, baggy bikinis with bras pulled tight across pancake-flat chests. In the background of several photos, another girl is lounging on a reclining chair. Her legs are long, her bikini stuffed to voluptuous adult proportions; she looks for all the world like the gorgeous college-age big sister of the birthday girl, perhaps home for the weekend to help little sis celebrate. It was Dark Rose.

"That was the problem," Dark Rose murmured, closing the photo album and leaning back on the couch. "When I got to that age, I had no friends. The other girls didn't like me. I don't know if a man could understand, but I started my period when I was ten. I had to wear a bra when I was eight. In junior high I looked as old as the teachers. I was a lonely child. It's odd that now I'm twenty-seven, and I probably look younger than I did when I was twelve."

Dark Rose was adopted as an infant by a couple who lived in Southern California. If she knew anything about her biological parents, she didn't tell us. Her adoptive mother and father had a grown daughter and a young son they'd adopted earlier.

One of her earliest memories involves drinking blood.

"The blood-drinking probably started when I was four years old," Dark Rose recalled. "I wouldn't cut myself on purpose, but when I did cut myself I automatically wanted the blood. It wasn't anything out in the open. I couldn't go around asking other people if I could have their blood. But I always knew I wanted it."

Any chance she had of a normal childhood, Dark Rose said, ended when her adoptive father molested her.

"He only did it one time, when I was six or seven," she said. "But that was enough. I didn't say anything at the time. I did later on. He and my mother divorced when I was eight. My mother was a very strict Baptist. She made me go to church until I was eleven, when I refused to do it anymore. I didn't have friends, I didn't have a real good family relationship, so I ended up spending a lot of time in the library. When I discovered spellbooks I read them all, and by the time I was thirteen I was a practicing, full-blown witch."

By the time she was thirteen, Dark Rose had also quit school and left home. School palled because the other girls ignored her, mostly, she thinks, because the boys all clustered around her.

"The funny thing is, I had then and still have a terrible self-image about my looks," Dark Rose confessed. "My mother even let me get some glamour shots taken—here's one; I'm twelve—to boost my confidence. But it didn't help."

At the time, Dark Rose was living with her mother and brother in Seattle. She'd spent the previous year visiting her father and his new family in California. She finished the ninth grade there, which marked the end of her formal education. But when Dark Rose found that she preferred the company of black boys, her father sent her back to Seattle.

Her mother didn't approve of her suitors' ethnicity there, either.

"If the boys were black, they couldn't call the house, nothing like that," Dark Rose said. "I felt completely unloved, which was wrong, because except for that racist thing I had a totally loving mother. She's a wonderful, wonderful person, but I guess growing up I knew I was different—the blood thing, for one—and I didn't want to change to become popular with the other kids. Finally, it got so bad at school, I was so socially inept, that they called in my mother and told her it would probably be better if I didn't come to class anymore and just got my G.E.D. And Mom told me okay, but I couldn't just hang around the house all day, I had to go out and find a job."

So thirteen-year-old Dark Rose headed for the nearest mall.

"I spent my days just sitting there and not trying very hard to get a job," she said. "Then this black guy came up to me and started talking. He was a man who really seemed nice. I was thirteen, I looked twenty, I was insecure, naive in the street sense and the world sense. I was a virgin still, he was the person I was de-virginized with. Not a pleasant experience, but he said he loved me and would take care of me. My mother said she knew what I was doing, and I couldn't live in her house and do that. So I turned to Ricky. He lived at home, but he put me up in a house with a couple of his other girls. He was a pimp. So yeah, I was a prostitute."

Dark Rose was interrupted by the appearance of her oldest child, whom she briskly ordered out of the room because she was talking. The child went over to Avery, who asked about lunch and went into the kitchen to fix something to eat.

(During our interview, Dark Rose was remarkably candid about her children, who, as you'll learn, suffered all sorts of trauma along with their mother. A week later, though, she called and asked us not to mention the kids by name, or to give their genders or specific ages.)

Dark Rose didn't enjoy being a hooker. But her mother wouldn't take her back, and she had no place else to go, so she stayed with Ricky. The other prostitutes in his stable didn't prove any friendlier than the girls she had known in school.

"They were obviously older than I was," she said. "We didn't really talk about our goals or dreams or anything. We talked about the customers, we talked about pimps, what we really thought of them. And we talked about, 'Yeah, we don't really want to be doing this.' Ricky had me working on First Street in Seattle. There was a club called Paradise Alley, Paradise Club, something like that. When I was fourteen I started to strip there besides working on the street."

It was a hard life. At one point Dark Rose left Ricky for another pimp named Craig, who promptly sold her back to Ricky.

"This is how bad my self-image was," she said. "I kind of liked it because I thought it proved I was worth something if Ricky was willing to pay for me."

Things came to a head a few months later. Dark Rose had broken away from Ricky and was working on her own, still as a prostitute. She was in touch with her mother, who would bring her food if she had nothing to eat. Dark Rose was living in a dingy motel. One day the motel janitor broke into her room and raped her. When she reported the rape to the police, they refused to do anything about it.

"Their attitude was: 'You're a prostitute, so if somebody rapes you it doesn't matter,'" she said bitterly. "I didn't know what to do next, so I called my mother. She told me I had to leave Seattle, try to get back to a normal life, or she wouldn't have anything to do with me. So she sent me to California to live with my father."

That didn't work out too well. Dark Rose arrived with ambivalent feelings about her father. Because the sexual abuse had only occurred once, she felt he wouldn't try that again. He greeted her when she arrived at his home in Torrance with the news that she had to go out and find a job since she wasn't attending school.

"Of course I couldn't go back to school," Dark Rose remembered. "After the way I'd been living, the things I'd done to survive, what would I possibly have in common with a bunch of little teenagers?"

Halfheartedly looking for a job, Dark Rose had plenty of time to dwell on her continuing fascination with the occult and her urge to drink human blood.

"I was still interested in blood-drinking, but I also still didn't know how to approach it," she said. "What I had learned to do was to take a person's lifeforce essence. My first instinct was to take blood, but I didn't yet know how to do that. I started taking lifeforce before I left home in Seattle, before Ricky, probably when I was twelve. It was with a person named Mark, who lived somewhere in my neighborhood. He was two or three years older, but he was nice to me. Mark was blond and blue-eyed, not usually the type of person I'm attracted to, but I couldn't get over the fact he really didn't want anything from me. He thought it was cool that I was different from everybody else, and he just wanted to talk to me. So I attached to him real quickly. He also, of course, wanted to kiss me and touch me, so I believe we were at his house, outside the garage, either that or at the bus stop. He came to kiss me, and I just grabbed his face and—well, unless I do it to you, it's hard to explain. You open your mouth like you're going to kiss someone, but you don't kiss them. You just inhale and the person is just depleted a little bit. It was the first time I did it. I didn't even know what I was doing, I just wanted to take something more of him than a kiss. Mark didn't know what was happening to him. It made me feel good. It made me feel like for the first time I had an edge over a person, yet it wasn't like I was hurting him. After that, I'd experiment with taking lifeforce from other people every once in a while, but it wasn't until five or six years ago that I began doing it regularly."

Dark Rose never did find a job in Torrance. Instead, she found Brad, another pimp.

"It was at a mall again, and I guess I just had a habit of meeting the wrong people," she said. "I was fifteen, I guess, but I looked older and dressed older, and Brad came along and everything started up again. It was bad at home because I'd confronted my father about molesting me, and everybody was calling me a liar. So when Brad said, 'You can come and live with me, and you don't have to do anything,' I went. I really think he meant that, but his other girlfriend who lived with him had to work on the street, and she told him that if I didn't have to work, too, then she was leaving. Some bad things happened. I started working for a couple of weeks. We girls would go out in groups to nightclubs where we could find guys. One night we picked up a bunch of guys, and for some reason they decided to pick on me. They held a gun to me and told me to take off all my clothes and jewelry. I had to do that; the other girls didn't. So I was naked in their car, and we had to stop at a gas station because they needed gas. I was sitting there naked in a bright gas station. It was very humiliating."

After a few weeks, Dark Rose told Brad she didn't want to be a prostitute anymore. He dumped her in a bad neighborhood, where she was taken in for a couple of months by an older man named Lawrence. Then Dark Rose made contact with her father, who told her that a warrant had been issued for her arrest.

"I'd been shoplifting," she said matter-of-factly. "My father took me into court and asked the judge to release me in his custody, but I was put into juvenile hall for six months. I didn't fit in there. I wasn't a gangster. I was so alone. Eventually I got used to it, but I was happy when they let me out. I'd been in for six months, but it felt like ten years. I don't remember anybody there trying to counsel me or anything. I had gonorrhea when they put me there, and

I'm surprised I didn't have anything else. So, about juvenile hall I remember being sick and eating the meals and not much else."

Released into her father's custody, Dark Rose was placed in a high school program for problem kids. She wasn't there long. One day she was standing just inside the school's fence and a black guy attending an adjacent community college walked by. They talked that day and the next. She began skipping school to hang out with him.

"Kevin became my first husband, and if I hate anybody at all, he's probably who it is," Dark Rose said. "At first he was really nice to me, but then he wanted to have sex and I didn't, and he raped me. I told him after that I didn't want to have anything to do with him, but then a couple of months later I knew I was pregnant, and he had to be the father. I hadn't had sex with anybody else. When I told my father I was pregnant, he said I'd have to have an abortion, but I didn't want to. I went into this maternity home with the plan of having the baby and giving it up for adoption."

Dark Rose wanted nothing to do with Kevin, though he knew she was pregnant because she'd seen him and talked to him a few times. Her father told her that after she'd given her baby up he'd get her an apartment and send her to college, but she went into premature labor and her baby was delivered by cesarean section. The adoption plan still hadn't been completed—there was no family waiting for the baby. Dark Rose's father wouldn't take her back if the baby was part of the package, so she called Kevin.

"He told me he'd really straightened out, and that the baby and I should come live with him and his mother," Dark Rose said. "It was horrible. He was abusive to me, his mother was abusive to me. I broke away for a while, and the welfare system put me in protective custody, which means they got me a motel, and I could pay for it with vouchers. Kevin finally found me and took the baby. He eventually raped me again, and I got pregnant again."

During the three years of her on-again, off-again relationship with Kevin, Dark Rose began thinking more about blood-drinking.

"I was dying to do it," she said. "Maybe I could have done some of it when I was a prostitute, but thank God, I didn't. I talked a little bit about it to Kevin, asking him what he thought of witchcraft, but it never went further than that. The spells and things I did, I did totally in private, and because of that I was not being who I wanted to be. I had met a girl named Gina in the maternity home, and she became my first real friend. Sometimes when I was with her I would secretly experience the lifeforce intake. And it was with Gina, also, that I realized I was bisexual. Until then I really didn't know I was. I never told Gina about the lifeforce or witchcraft or blood-drinking or bisexuality because her family was strict Christian. Just in natural female closeness I was able to take the lifeforce, and I don't think she ever realized."

Dark Rose left Kevin again during her second pregnancy. He kept their first child; she said he didn't care about the second one.

"I tried to get visitation, but they wouldn't let me," she said. "Well, I got off welfare and got a job at another strip bar, but as a waitress. I met Eric then. He was somebody I could talk to, and I never felt he judged me. I told him things I was interested in, and he had no problem. And so, finally, one time in the heat of passion I told him I wanted to cut him and drink his blood and his reaction was, 'Cool, let's try this.'"

Dark Rose's first attempts at blood-drinking involved a lot of trial and error.

"My favorite place to cut, now that I've had experience, is on the chest, right above the nipple, right there," she said, gesturing at her own chest. "It's a sexual place to me, and it's accessible. There was the inner thigh, of course, and I was tempted to do that, but there's the femoral artery there, and I didn't know what

I was doing, exactly. So I picked the safe place on the chest. I was a little bit nervous, cutting somebody's flesh, so it wasn't major gushes of blood or anything. I just went down like this"—she made a quick, cutting gesture—"and it trickled down and I drank it, and that was enough."

Afterward, Dark Rose thought about what had happened.

"It's not like blood tastes really good," she recalled. "I don't think it has any nutritional value or anything. But I was licking up Eric's blood. His blood is what kept him alive. So when I was doing it, it was totally erotic and sexual, and this person was under me doing what I said to do. I had power over this person. I was drinking his blood, for God's sake, and he didn't dislike it. For him, it wasn't an awful experience."

Her initial reaction to drinking blood never changed.

"Actually, drinking blood is a sexual, erotic experience," she explained. "You become this animal, this entity. You can let down all the barriers society has put on you, all the things you're supposed to think, the way you're supposed to behave. At that moment when I take the blood, I totally feel like a Dark Angel. That's how I describe myself, and that's how I feel. That first time with Eric was such a release. I'd tasted my own blood and thought somebody else's might taste different. It didn't. The joy was the whole predator thing. I don't know if it was because I'd been victimized all my life, but I loved the power of it. I totally enjoyed it and loved it, and that was that. I was going to keep on doing it."

But she didn't keep on doing it with Eric. They broke up after she drank his blood a few more times during sex. Dark Rose wasn't alone long. She got something going with Manuel, the manager-bouncer of the strip bar where she worked as a waitress, and also became friends with Avery, a frequent customer there. But her relationship with him was platonic. She moved in with Manuel, and eventually married him. Her youngest child, who lived with them, called Manuel "Daddy."

"By this time I was much stronger about who I was and what I believed," Dark Rose said. "Some books on witchcraft were coming out, and I read them. And I felt confident approaching Manuel about what I wanted to do, meaning drink his blood. At that time, though, I never used the word 'vampire,' never used the term 'vampirism.' It hadn't entered my mind yet that that's what I was."

Manuel was game for anything, Dark Rose said, as long as she swore whatever they were doing wasn't satanic.

"He was a good Catholic," she laughed. "I explained Satan had nothing to do with it. After that, whatever I wanted to do was all right with him as long as it was sexual. I couldn't just walk up to him and say, 'Hey, can I have some blood?' But when we had sex, maybe every third time, he'd let me have blood. That kept me attached to him longer than I otherwise would have been."

We were interrupted by Dark Rose's youngest child, who complained about a splinter in a finger.

"I'm talking," Dark Rose said, not raising her voice but leaving no room for protest, either. "Go ask Avery to get it out." The child went off and called Avery "Daddy" when requesting help getting the splinter out.

"I was together with Manuel for four years," Dark Rose resumed. "I was never in love with him, but he had kind of rescued me. He wanted to take care of me and my youngest child. The only way Kevin would divorce me was if he had custody of our first child, so I got the divorce and also visitation rights. Manuel and I got married. He was very good to me and loving and kind and understanding and accepting. That was something I hadn't had, and I wasn't going to throw it away. But I set the terms of our relationship. It was absolutely one-sided, very unhealthy."

Manuel encouraged Dark Rose to quit her job at the bar. Since she didn't have to work anymore, she started keeping hours that felt comfortable to her.

"I was never a day person," she said. "Now I could be up all night and take some time to think things through. I started thinking about vampirism, but 'vampire' to me just felt so cheesy and commercial. But over the last three years, really, I've been more accepting of it. It was gradual. I kept thinking, 'Maybe what I'm doing is vampirism,' but I didn't say it aloud to Manuel."

But she did say it aloud to Avery, who had become a close friend.

"He was in the bar all the time, and I knew he loved me," she said. "I wouldn't do anything that way with him because I was married to Manuel, and because I wouldn't let myself feel attracted to Avery sexually. But I could talk to him in a way I couldn't with Manuel, because after a while I found out Manuel wasn't really all right about the blood-drinking and witchcraft. He was just accepting of them because he didn't want to lose me. And yet Avery would come to me and say, 'You need to pursue what you really are. You're getting ready to come into your full spiritual being.' I finally got the nerve to say to him, 'Okay, this is what I am. I am a vampire, not in the commercial sense, but being a vampire is what I do. I am also a practicing witch.'

"And Avery's reaction was, 'Uh-huh, and your point is?' So through Avery I felt myself coming into my full being."

About the same time, Dark Rose regained custody of her oldest child. Kevin's mother died, Kevin himself went to jail for a while, so Dark Rose simply took the six-year-old home with her and Manuel.

Marriage to Manuel didn't work out. He resented Dark Rose's continuing friendship with Avery, who told her frankly that he was in love with her. Still, the relationship between Dark Rose and Avery remained platonic—through her choice.

"Most of the time I was married to Manuel, I would live with my kids at Avery's," she said. "Now, Avery let it be known he was much better for me than Manuel and that I should be with him. But I kept telling Avery that yes, I loved him, but no, I wasn't physically attracted to him, and romance between us was not going to happen. And I'd go back and live with Manuel for a while, and that would get bad, and I'd go to Avery and back to Manuel, and finally Avery got sick of it."

Avery went to dinner with Dark Rose and told her he was through with her.

"Suddenly I thought, 'Can I live without him the rest of my life?' And it was like a burst of energy in me," she said. "He'd been trying to get me to kiss him for years, and so I did, and it was like this wall came down, and I was attracted to him after all. I left Manuel for Avery. It was simple, in the end."

The new relationship wasn't vampirically simple, though. Manuel had been willing to let Dark Rose drink his blood. Avery, though he supported his new fiancée's right to believe whatever she wanted, wasn't sure he was ready to become her blood donor.

Even if he had decided he wanted to try, Dark Rose found herself reticent.

"If Avery and I were together, and he was my donor, that would be ideal, but I have some hinky problem of doing it with him, and I don't know what it is," she said. "It's because I'm in love with him, I guess. And when I'm being a vampire, I'm a predator, and the person is my victim even though I'm not really hurting him. I'm in power, and I'm sort of victimizing the person to get what I want. Avery's actually said many times, 'Fine, do it, sure,' and I'm like, 'Okay, great,' and I can't."

That dilemma was compounded when Avery, Dark Rose, and her children moved from Los Angeles to Orlando. He had his writing; she had plenty of spare time to reflect on how much she hated living in Florida.

"We had some relationship problems because I was totally disoriented," Dark Rose said. "Financially things weren't good for a while, either."

Also, Dark Rose found herself without a regular blood donor after several years of steady blood-drinking with Manuel.

"If I don't get blood regularly, then I definitely miss it, miss it very much," she said. "I get more negative than usual, and I'm naturally very moody anyway. When I don't have a donor, I'm more prone to get into arguments. When I have a donor, I'm more positive."

Dark Rose's blood withdrawal ended when she met a young woman who shared her interest in Wicca.

"She was younger, twenty-one, and not judgmental," Dark Rose said. "I thought I should take blood from a woman because of the boundaries of my relationship with Avery. To me, drinking blood is always an erotic thing, and I didn't feel it would be right to do it with a man. With this woman, it wasn't like I was cheating or anything. Avery knew about it; when I did it with her we weren't naked. I took it from her wrist, usually. But no matter how I tried with her it was still erotic, still sexual, and I don't know how to do it and not have it be that way."

Still, Dark Rose continued her donor relationship with the young woman until the end of 1995.

"It finally didn't work anymore," she said. "That was the first time I'd had blood from a woman, and it's certainly something I could do again."

By the time Dark Rose ended her relationship with the Florida donor, though, she had other things on her mind. Soon after arriving in Orlando, Avery subscribed to America Online. Dark Rose, who said she's otherwise "an antitechnical person," logged on, discovered vampire chat rooms, and couldn't tear herself away from the computer keyboard.

"I was thrilled with it for about a week, then realized all those people were in an Anne Rice fantasy," she said. "That's when I got the idea to start the journal, to let people share the fantasies and adventures of true vampires, or Dark Angels as I prefer to call myself. 'Vampire' is just the closest common phrase most people would understand. I told Avery, 'I'm just going to write about what I do, what I believe, my philosophy. And if I get enough subscribers, maybe this will be something good for us to share.'"

Dark Rose began by purchasing a subscription to the *Vampire Information Exchange*, and by reading *Vampires Among Us*, from which she gleaned more organizational addresses. Some of the publications she began receiving had addresses of new members, which Dark Rose turned into her own mailing list. Avery's writing and computer design skills combined well with Dark Rose's self-described "vampire erotica." From the first issue, *The Dark Rose Journal* was a success; to date it's covering production and mailing costs. If its subscriber base continues to expand, Avery's goal of turning it into a slick newsstand periodical might be realized.

Dark Rose has gloried in all her new correspondents.

"I have all these people writing to me," she said happily. "I wasn't prepared for the response I got. It was overwhelming. From the first issue on, people said they could notice the difference between *The Dark Rose Journal* and everything else. They were dying for the things that were in there. My goal now is for it to be on the news-stands. A month ago, we did a photo shoot in a cemetery. We weren't doing anything wrong, we weren't hurting anyone, but we got kicked out because of the way we looked. People kept berating us because we looked like a bunch of vampires. There's so much prejudice."

By "us," Dark Rose meant a new group of friends she'd assembled in Orlando called "The Dark Court." It consists of local subscribers to *The Dark Rose Journal* who join her periodically for discussions, photo sessions for reproduction in later *Journals*, and perhaps, eventually, blood-drinking.

"I'm working on finding a new blood donor for myself, see-ing a lot of my Dark Court on a regular basis," she explained. "I'm kind of scoping out everyone in it to be sure I'll have some-one I want. Before I take someone's blood, I want a bond there. There has to be trust. But I'm going to find another donor. I have to. I can't turn back. Oh, I could live and survive without blood, of course, but I don't want to. I have many offers on the table. I'll prefer it to be a female because I'm in a relationship, and it's more acceptable for me to be with a female, because Avery has no prob-lem with that. He'd probably like to watch, I'm sure. But right now, my offers are all male."

In this non-blood-drinking interim, Dark Rose has turned to Avery. She said she takes his lifeforce regularly, almost always while he's sleeping. That's enough to tide her over—for now.

Dark Rose candidly described her technique for blood-drink-ing, the one she's used with all past donors and will follow with her future ones.

"You don't have to cut very deep," she said. "I don't want a gush of blood—no, I take that back. I would like a lot of blood, but people don't want you to do that, really. I usually cut with a razor blade, about two inches, and deep enough to where the blood is running down them. Sometimes I've left a couple of scars. I don't want to leave donors scarred. Still, it's deeper than a scratch."

Mostly, Dark Rose said, the bleeding stops before she's really been able to drink her fill.

"Afterward I wipe the cut off and put Neosporin on it," she said. "If it hasn't stopped bleeding by the time I'm done sucking or licking it up, I put on a Band-Aid. And always, always, I make sure it's something the other person is willing to do. If someone said, 'I don't want to do this,' I wouldn't do it."

Blood, Dark Rose said, "tastes pretty coppery and not quite bitter. If you want to see what it tastes like without taking real blood, mix V-8 Juice with orange juice and leave it to warm to room temperature."

❧

It got dark outside. Dark Rose's children came in for good, trailing bikes and muddy shoes. We ordered pizza delivered and some buffalo wings because Dark Rose's oldest child especially liked them.

"I'm very open with my children about myself, what's happened to me and what I am," Dark Rose said. "My youngest child in lots of ways reminds me of myself; I think we must have been related in another life."

Avery finally came to join us in the living room. He talked a little about Dark Rose, her vampirism, and his reaction to it.

"I opened my mind to the fact that the world is made up of many millions of kinds of beliefs and lifestyles, and that one is not necessarily superior to all the others," he mused, his bulky body sprawled on the couch next to Dark Rose's slender silhouette. "If drinking blood is part of her beliefs and her life, then I can't change that, nor would I wish to."

His fiancée has never pressured him to let her drink his blood, he added.

"If Dark Rose were to say to me, 'Gee, honey, I think we need to do this because we can't have a relationship unless you get on board here,' well, she hasn't," Avery said. "I'm not saying that in the future I might not lean more in that direction, but I have no inclination toward it right now."

What Avery really wanted to talk about was *The Dark Rose Journal*. Which stories did we like best? Which ones could have been written better? His own background as a writer was obviously extensive; he was familiar with many obscure authors and was self-confident enough to invite constructive criticism of his own work.

Just before the pizza arrived, a member of Dark Rose's Dark Court rang the doorbell. She'd invited Aaron to meet us, she said, because he seemed to be her spiritual equal, and a fellow Wiccan. Earlier, she'd said Aaron might be the first person she would ever allow to drink her blood "because there's a balance between us."

Aaron joined Dark Rose and Avery on the couch. She sat between the two men. Aaron was quite young, in his early twenties and good-looking. When Dark Rose and Avery excused themselves for a few minutes, we asked Aaron about Wiccan beliefs. Despite Dark Rose's high praise for him, he seemed to have trouble articulating what he believed and why he believed it.

"In the Dark Court, Aaron is the master and I'm the mistress," Dark Rose said as she came back into the living room. "He's the master because he's the only one in that circle who is really the same as I am. Everybody else just wants to hang out. There's a difference. The rest of the Dark Court are just people, cool, nice people. They're into Goth, but they're not like Aaron and I are. I totally try to stay away from the kids in capes. We had a meeting with the Dark Court people and I said, 'This is exactly what I do not want. Do not come in vampire makeup.' Most of the girls already had jet-black hair, so I said that was fine. My hair is dyed black, but I did that because Avery wanted me to. But I told them not to come with black lipstick on, don't come dressed like the undead, that's not what we're about. I want to have a dark court of dark angels with everyone being sexy and erotic."

When the pizza was delivered, Avery took the children into the kitchen and put out plates for them. Dark Rose's oldest child had brought along a friend who stayed for dinner. While Avery fussed with the kids, Dark Rose and Aaron huddled together on the couch, planning some activity for the Dark Court.

Just before we left, we asked Dark Rose how she would change her past if she could.

She looked up from her conversation with Aaron and said flatly, "I'd never change my life. The pain made me who I am. I don't blame anybody for what happened to me. You have to take responsibility for everything that happens in your life. I am so proud of myself and the way I think and the way I look at life. I would go through everything again to get to where I am. I would."

In the kitchen, Avery told the kids not to eat too fast. Dark Rose and Aaron began talking quietly again. Only a full moon illuminated the pitch-black night as we drove away.

# Afterword:
## Something in the Blood

Everything you've just read is factual, at least in the way we've recorded what was told to us by the various vampires, blood-drinkers, and vampire victims. There's no way to know, of course, whether any of them were exaggerating things or even making up whole parts of their stories during our interviews with them. What we can tell you with absolute certainty is that we've done our best to serve as conduits, not interpreters. What they had to say is what you've seen on these pages.

We taped all of the interviews, except one with Cayne Presley when our recorder didn't work. The tapes are backed up with our notes, and when we weren't sure what someone specifically said, we called back to confirm that we had the facts right.

Each person prominently featured—Martin Riccardo, Liriel McMahon, Gremlin, Victoria, Cayne Presley, Christine Darque, Michelle Belanger, Vlad, Avery, and Dark Rose—was interviewed in person, not over the phone or by fax. "Victoria" is a pseudonym. "Christine Darque" chose that name for herself. "Vlad" is, of course, a stage name. We never found out Gremlin's real name, but then we never asked him. "Dark Rose," "Avery," "Butch," and "Malcolm" are pseudonyms. The other names are, so far as we know, real ones.

Each vampire organization and publication is identified by its proper name. In an appendix, we're including those addresses as well as the addresses of Liriel, Gremlin, Cayne, Christine, Vlad, and Dark Rose, who said we could print them. We're not encouraging you write to anyone, but now you've got the necessary information if it's something you want to do.

All the photos were supplied to us by the people in them. Gremlin gave us the original design of his "Gremlin" tattoo.

After many months and thousands of miles, the obvious question for us is, "Do *you* believe in vampires?" It's tough to answer.

We *don't* believe in the superhuman vampire found in most movies and books. That undead creature doesn't exist, never has existed, never will exist. Forget it.

But if you define "vampire" as a human being who is compelled to drink the blood of other human beings, then, yes, vampires do exist. There are thousands of them in this country. Maybe, as Vlad believes, they're reincarnated souls who drink blood to have a better connection through memory with their past lives. Maybe, as Dark Rose insists, they're superior beings, the top of the food chain, who think and feel things the rest of us don't because of their blood intake. Maybe, as Martin Riccardo has decided, they're just expressing a sexual blood fetish. Or maybe, like Cayne Presley suggests, they just do it because it feels so good.

Don't worry about being attacked by a blood-crazed vampire. They can find willing donors. If you aren't willing, there's no reason to go around protecting your neck, which isn't the body area where vampires feed anyway. Still, chances are good you've met a vampire or three without knowing it. Maybe, after reading this book, every once in a while you'll find yourself wondering who that person or persons might be. If you did find out, you'd probably be surprised. It's practically certain Victoria's customers at her department store lingerie counter don't have any idea the chubby girl waiting on them would like to drink a little of their blood. But she would. Can you be certain you don't know any Victorias?

The bottom line is this: No matter what *you* believe, no matter what *we* believe, the people you've read about here do believe in blood-drinking, do believe in vampirism. And, like all of us, they act in accordance with their beliefs.

They have to, because there's something in the blood.

# *Appendices*

---

## APPENDIX A
## THE INTERNATIONAL SOCIETY OF VAMPIRES'
## DECLARATION OF INTENT

*We are there, in every country, in every age. We suffer through the endless nights, alone but yearning for some form of companionship. For years we have instinctively sought one another out, exchanging extensive correspondence on our thoughts, our experiences, our personal beliefs. From that correspondence, the International Society of Vampires was born. The society answers our need for companionship, keeping us in contact with others who share our interests, our passions, our darkling obsessions.*

*We are the eternal. We are the hidden.*

*We are the vampires, and we invite you to join us through the march of endless nights.*

c/o Shadowfox Publications, P.O. Box 474, Hinckley, Ohio 44233

## APPENDIX   B
THE VAMPIRE CREED

*I am a vampire.*

*I worship my ego and I worship my life, for I am the only God that is.*

*I am proud that I am a predatory animal and I honor my animal instincts.*

*I exalt my rational mind and hold no belief that is in defiance of reason.*

*I recognize the difference between the worlds of truth and fantasy.*

*I acknowledge the fact that survival is the highest law.*

*I acknowledge the Powers of Darkness to be hidden natural laws through which I work my magic.*

*I know that my beliefs in Ritual are fantasy but the magic is real, and I respect and acknowledge the results of my magic.*

*I realize there is no heaven as there is no hell, and I view death as the destroyer of life.*

*Therefore I will make the most of life here and now.*

*I am a vampire.*

*Bow down before me.*

c/o Temple of the Vampire, Box 3582, Lacey, Washington 98503

## APPENDIX C
## SHADOWFOX SURVEY

Michelle Belanger recently conducted a residence survey of subscribers to various Shadowfox publications. Here is her breakdown of the ten states with the highest number of respondents, which she believes is roughly equivalent to a ranking of states with the highest vampire populations.

## STATE PERCENTAGE OF RESPONSE

| State | Percentage of Response |
|---|---|
| California | 15 percent |
| Washington | 12 percent |
| Ohio | 12 percent |
| Pennsylvania | 10 percent |
| Illinois | 8 percent |
| Texas | 8 percent |
| Florida | 8 percent |
| New York | 6 percent |
| Massachusetts | 5 percent |
| Indiana | 3 percent |

## APPENDIX D
ADDRESSES

For more information about vampirism, contact any of the
  following people or organizations:

Cayne Presley
9851 Jericho
El Paso, TX 79927

Christine Darque
3622-A Wingate Terrace
Indianapolis, IN 46236

*The Dark Rose Journal*
8879 W. Colonial Drive, Ste. 107
Ocoee, FL 34761

Screem Jams Productions Inc.
P.O. Box 138300
Chicago, IL 60613
E-mail: screem19@starnetinc.com
(Note: This is published by Vlad.)

Vampires of America
P.O. Box 771321
Wichita, KS 67277-1321

The Temple of the Vampire
Box 3582
Lacey, WA 98503

Shadowfox Publications
P.O. Box 474
Hinckley, OH 44233

Vampirism Research Institute
P.O. Box 21067
Seattle, WA 98111-3067
E-mail: LirielMc@aol.com

OTHER SUMMIT BOOKS BY JEFF GUINN

Nonfiction:

- *You Can't Hit the Ball With the Bat on Your Shoulder: The Baseball Life and Times of Bobby Bragan* (with Bobby Bragan)

- *Sometimes A Fantasy: Midlife Misadventures with Baseball Heroes*

Fiction:

- *The Autobiography of Santa Claus: It's Better to Give*